COOKIE CLASS

120 IRRESISTIBLE DECORATING
IDEAS FOR ANY OCCASION

JENNY KELLER

HARPER
DESIGN
An Imprint of HarperCollins Publishers

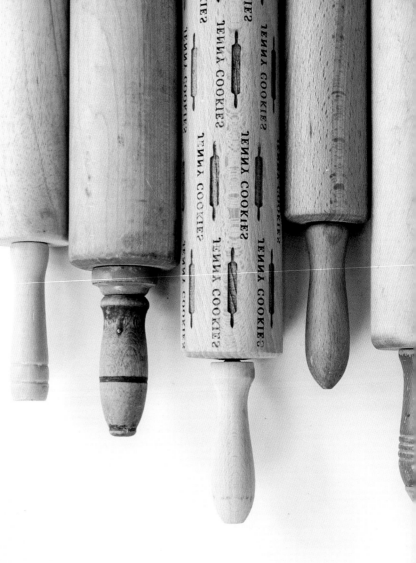

HarperCollins books may be purchased
for educational, business, or sales
promotional use. For information please
email the Special Markets Department
at SPsales@harpercollins.com.

First published in 2019 by
Harper Design
An Imprint of HarperCollins *Publishers*
195 Broadway
New York, NY 10007
Tel: (212) 207-7000
Fax: (855) 746-6023
harperdesign@harpercollins.com
www.hc.com

Distributed throughout the world by
HarperCollins *Publishers*
195 Broadway
New York, NY 10007

ISBN 978-0-06-289848-7
Library of Congress Control Number:
2018965792

Book design by Sarah Gifford

Printed in China
First Printing, 2019

To my Aunt Susan,
who always let me bake in her kitchen,
no matter how big the mess.

Contents

FALL

WINTER

Introduction

The first time I ever baked cookies was with my grandmother when I was two years old. I sat on her kitchen counter and watched as she correctly measured flour, tapping the cup and scraping the excess flour flush off the top with a knife. According to family lore, when she asked me to dump the flour into the mixing bowl, I eagerly emptied the flour-filled measuring cup into the pocket of her bathrobe, instead of pouring the flour into the bowl.

I have always loved baking. To me, it is more than making a dessert. It's a way to be creative and satisfy my award-winning sweet tooth. Baking has added an element of connection to the many layers of my life—as a child, with my family; in college, with my friends; and later, at a pivotal moment in my life, with my daughter.

In 2006, my husband came home from work and handed me a cookbook with a recipe that promised to make the best sugar cookies ever. Not owning a single cookie tool or ingredient, I found myself at our local craft store searching for any and all cookie-related merchandise. I remember tossing an orange plastic pumpkin-shaped cookie cutter into my shopping cart and thinking, "Pumpkins it is!"

At home, I put my daughter, Ally, who was six months old at the time, in her high chair with a few wooden spoons to bang. I grabbed an apron, and decided to give cookie making a try. The results were disappointing. The cookies were bland and lacked flavor.

Not one to back down from a challenge, I was still inspired to make a truly delicious sugar cookie. My in-laws kindly shared a sugar cookie recipe with me but it only included a list of ingredients. I was

determined to make it my own, a cookie I could proudly share with family and friends.

The process was a little rough around the edges. I didn't have a set of directions or the tips and tools needed, just a list of ingredients with a baking temperature. The second batch turned out a million times better than the first. Eventually, I got the hang of it and soon became hooked on baking sugar cookies. I baked them almost every day, perfecting the recipe as I went along. I handed cookies out to family, friends, neighbors, and even people I'd just met. I loved the holidays, making pumpkin-shaped cookies for Halloween, turkey cookies at Thanksgiving, and snowflake and angel cookies for Christmas.

Baking became a creative outlet. The cookies were my palette and the buttercream was my paint. I loved that there were no limits. I could blend colors and create textured surfaces as I liked. I could dream up an original cookie design for any season or celebration.

My friends and family loved the cookies and began to refer to them as "Jenny Cookies." The cookies were requested at every family gathering, social event, and party. Friends of friends began asking for cookies. Soon enough I was baking for nearly everyone I knew.

After about two years, I was making so many cookies that people kept suggesting I open a storefront. I wasn't ready for that just yet. Instead, I launched my blog, JennyCookies.com, to share my creations with others. I also added cupcakes, cakes, and mini-desserts to the mix. Before I knew it, I had fans all over the world.

As the demand for Jenny Cookies increased, friends and acquaintances began asking for baking lessons. Lunch dates with girlfriends turned into cookie-making sessions in my kitchen, so I decided to offer a cookie decorating class. I rented the kitchen at my children's preschool and announced the class on my Facebook page.

The class sold out in less than twenty-four hours. I had so much fun teaching the class that I offered a second. I ignited a cookie craze.

Jenny Cookies Bake Shop officially opened in December 2016, in my hometown, Lake Stevens, Washington, almost ten years after my first not-so-noteworthy batch. I almost pinched myself, standing behind the counter on opening day. The display case was filled with gorgeous cupcakes, cakes, mini-desserts, and, of course, Jenny Cookies. Alongside me was a team of talented bakers and decorators, friends and family, all eager to open the doors and welcome the line of customers wrapped around the building.

Over the years, the bake shop has become a destination bakery, and I regularly meet customers visiting from Washington and across the United States. While I've expanded my repertoire of desserts, buttercream sugar cookies continue to be the top seller.

I invite you to join me in the kitchen to bake my signature buttercream sugar cookies. The recipes are fail-proof; you'll master them quickly. Then the fun really begins. Put on an apron and grab a bowl. Let's bake!

Baking and Decorating Tools

Here are the tools I use in my kitchen. The items in the essential list will ensure a properly baked and decorated sugar cookie. The optional items—which include packaging and presentation elements—will allow you to take your baking and decorating to an advanced level.

ESSENTIAL

COOKIE CUTTERS IN VARIOUS SHAPES

DISPOSABLE DECORATING BAGS

HEAVY-DUTY, HIGH-SPEED STAND MIXER, OR A POWERFUL HAND MIXER WITH BEATER ATTACHMENT

MEASURING CUPS AND SPOONS

MIXING BOWLS

NONSTICK BAKING OR COOKIE SHEETS

PLASTIC WRAP

POTHOLDERS OR OVEN MITTS

ROLLING PIN

RUBBER OR PLASTIC SPATULAS

WILTON COUPLERS

WILTON DECORATING TIPS IN VARIOUS SIZES

WIRE COOLING RACKS

OPTIONAL

FOOD PROCESSOR FOR CHOPPING NUTS, CANDY CANES, AND OTHER DOUGH AND ICING MIX-INS

METAL SPATULA

MICROPLANE GRATER FOR ZESTING CITRUS FRUITS AND CHOCOLATE

MORTAR AND PESTLE FOR GRINDING HERBS, SPICES, AND EDIBLE FLOWERS

OFFSET ANGLED SPATULA

OVEN THERMOMETER

PAPER CUPCAKE LINERS FOR DISPLAYING COOKIES IN TINS AND BOXES

PARCHMENT PAPER

RIBBON AND BAKER'S TWINE FOR DECORATING

SHARP KNIVES

Making Cookie Dough

The list of ingredients on page 16 is all you need to make the most delicious sugar cookie dough. This recipe took me a while to perfect but if you follow my precise instructions your cookies will turn out great! Always begin with prepared ingredients and equipment and don't use substitutes; I only use real butter in my Jenny Cookies recipe. The key is using room-temperature butter! I only know of two ways for people to mess up my recipe: one, using butter that has been melted down in a microwave, and two, mismeasuring ingredients. Be sure to spend two to three minutes beating your sugar and butter. But as soon as the flour is added, keep mixing to a minimum. The more time you spend beating your dough, the denser the cookie will be. Keep it short and sweet! When adding mix-ins, stir them in by hand so that you don't overwork the dough. I also use pure extracts whenever possible as they yield the best flavor. For food coloring, AmeriColor gives my frostings a brilliant color without my having to use a lot.

These sprinkle ingredients are referenced throughout the recipes in the book and give my cookies a little extra flair. Sprinkles add an element of fun and can be used in several creative ways. (They also mask any decorating imperfections!)

RAINBOW OR CHOCOLATE SPRINKLES

EDIBLE GLITTER

QUINNS

PEARLS

SANDING SUGAR

My Sugar Cookie Dough Recipe

YIELD 36

YOU WILL NEED

4½ cups (576 g) all-purpose flour, plus more for rolling

1 tablespoon baking powder

1½ cups (3 sticks/340 g) salted butter, at room temperature

1½ cups (300 g) white granulated sugar

3 large eggs

1 tablespoon pure vanilla extract

VARIATION FOR GLUTEN-FREE (GF) COOKIES

Replace all-purpose flour with equal amounts of gluten-free flour such as Bob's Red Mill brand.

❶ Whisk the flour and baking powder together in a medium bowl.

❷ Beat the butter and sugar together in a large bowl with an electric mixer fitted with the paddle attachment on medium speed until smooth or about 2½ minutes. Beat in the eggs and vanilla until fluffy, about 1 minute. Scrape the sides of the bowl with a rubber spatula.

❸ Turn the mixer speed to low and add the flour mixture approximately a quarter at a time, scraping the sides of the bowl after each addition. The dough will form a ball around the paddle attachment and feel soft but not sticky.

❹ Wrap the dough ball in a piece of plastic wrap and press down to form a 1-inch (2.5-cm) thick disk. Refrigerate for at least 10 minutes, or store for up to 7 days tightly wrapped.

❺ Preheat the oven to 375°F (190°C).

❻ Roll out the dough on a lightly floured flat work surface to about ¼-inch (6-mm) thickness, using additional flour as necessary to prevent sticking. Use cookie cutters to create the shapes you want, and carefully transfer with a metal spatula to a nonstick baking sheet, placing the cookies about ¾ inch (1 cm) apart.

❼ Bake one sheet at a time on the middle rack about 7 to 8 minutes, until puffy. Let the cookies rest for 2 minutes before transferring to a wire rack to cool.

❽ Repeat steps 6 and 7 with the gathered scraps until all the dough has been used.

Rolling Out the Dough, Cutting, and Baking

Rolling Out the Dough

Before rolling out your dough, you'll want to make sure you have a nicely floured surface. This is one of the easiest tricks I share in my cookie class: Use a clean, damp paper towel and wipe your counter. Sprinkle the flour on the slightly damp counter to create a floured surface that won't shift under the dough when you roll it out.

When rolling dough, it is essential to keep the dough chilled. Once the dough is rolled out, work quickly to keep it cool to the touch. Cold dough cut-outs are easier to transfer to a baking sheet, and they hold their shape better. If your dough gets too warm, it can cause cookies to spread when baking and lose their shape. Return warm dough to the fridge until chilled before continuing.

Extra dough or dough made ahead of time can be refrigerated and saved for later. Wrap it by laying a piece of plastic wrap on the counter and placing the dough on the plastic. Wrap the plastic around the dough and flatten the dough pile into a 1-inch thick disk. Refrigerate for up to 7 days, or freeze for up to a month.

Cookie Cutting

With a little creativity, bakers can get by with just a few basic cookie cutters in generic shapes. If you're new to cookie decorating, there's no need to go overboard right away. Start small and build a collection.

Choose cookie cutters with minimal appendages to avoid breakage and burning while baking. Dip the cookie cutter into flour after every few cuts to ensure the cutter doesn't stick to the dough.

If you can't locate a specific cutter, you should be able to find a template online. Just print it out to the desired size and use it to cut the shape out of the dough with a paring knife.

Here's a list of basic cookie cutters to have in your arsenal:

PLAIN-EDGE ROUND CUTTERS

RUFFLED-EDGE ROUND CUTTERS

STARS

HEARTS

RECTANGLES

TRIANGLES

OVALS

SQUARES

TREES

SNOWFLAKES

SMALL AND LARGE LETTERS

NUMBERS

My favorite shops to look for cookie cutters are Etsy.com, Cheapcookiecutters.com, Wilton.com, JOANN, Williams-Sonoma, and Amazon.com.

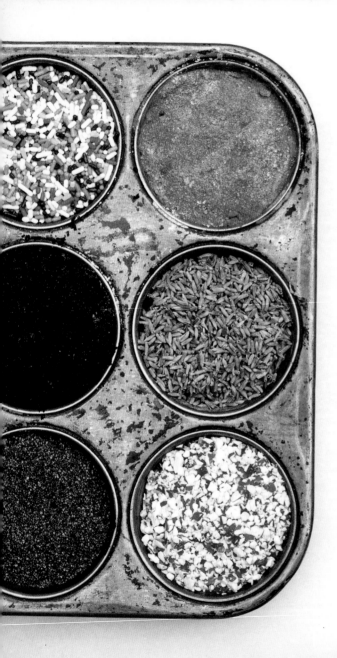

Baking the Cookies

It's time to bake! To eliminate extra cleanup, line baking pans with parchment paper. When transferring cookies to the baking pan, place them at least ½ inch (12 mm) apart to give the cookies plenty of room to bake evenly and not touch.

Be sure to bake only one tray at a time, unless you are baking in a convection oven. Baking multiple trays at once often leads to unevenly baked cookies. Use the middle rack for the most even heat.

The first time you bake the cookies, take a peek at them around the 6- or 7-minute mark. Every oven bakes a little differently, which is why I recommend a 7- to 9-minute baking time. You'll know they're done when they appear puffy. If you overbake them by a minute or two, they'll still taste good—they'll just be a bit crunchier. Let the cookies rest on the cookie sheet for about 2 minutes before transferring to a cooling rack.

SUGAR COOKIE DOUGH MIX-INS

Give your cookies a little extra flavor by experimenting with sugar cookie dough mix-ins! The measurements listed below are based on one standard batch of cookie dough. I don't recommend adding more than one mix-in per batch.

MINI CHOCOLATE CHIPS: 1 cup (198 g)

CRUSHED OREOS: 1 cup (100 g)

SPRINKLES: ½ cup (80 g)

DRIED EDIBLE FLOWERS: ¼ cup (10 g)

CHOPPED CANDY CANES: ½ cup (50 g)

COCOA POWDER: 1 cup (125 g)

CRANBERRIES: ½ cup (60 g)

PISTACHIOS: ½ cup (50 g)

PUMPKIN SPICE: 2 tablespoons cinnamon, 2 tablespoons allspice, 1 tablespoon nutmeg

INSTANT COFFEE: 1 cup (240 g)

CHOCOLATE COVERED PRETZELS: 1½ cups (90 g)

FOOD COLORING GEL: 1 to 2 drops

POPPY SEEDS: ¾ cup (95 g)

Making Buttercream Icing

The funny thing about my buttercream icing is, there's actually no butter in it! I use Imperial margarine because it yields the best results. It's easy to spread when piping and won't give your hand a cramp! I also use Imperial margarine because it's the lightest in color. If you desire a butterier taste, you can absolutely substitute butter for the margarine. Along with the margarine and confectioners' sugar, I use Crisco solid shortening, which allows my icing to form a light crust after drying. One of the most common questions I receive is about how I stack my cookies on trays or how I am able to package them in bags. Because my buttercream is a crusting buttercream, it makes packaging and stacking easy! After 6 to 8 hours, the icing will crust just enough for the cookies to be carefully packaged in cellophane bags or layered on a cake plate.

The last ingredient I want to talk about is clear vanilla extract. The clear vanilla ensures the icing stays white. Using regular vanilla will give your icing a creamy color, which is fine if you want your icing brown or another dark color. But if you are going for a pure white icing, you'll want to use the clear vanilla extract.

My Buttercream Icing Recipe

MAKES ABOUT 9 CUPS (2 KG)
PROVIDES ICING FOR ABOUT 36
STANDARD (3-INCH) COOKIES

YOU WILL NEED

1½ cups (3 sticks/340 g) butter
or margarine

1½ cups (310 g) vegetable
shortening

3 pounds (1.4 kg) confectioners'
sugar (about 10½ to 11 cups)

1 tablespoon clear vanilla extract

¼ cup (60 ml) heavy cream

❶ Combine the butter and shortening in the bowl of an electric mixer.

❷ Using the paddle attachment, beat on medium speed until smooth, about 2 minutes.

❸ Add half of the confectioners' sugar and continue beating on low speed for an additional 2 minutes, or until the mixture is creamy, scraping the sides of the bowl with a rubber spatula as needed. Add the remaining confectioners' sugar, vanilla, and heavy cream, and beat until the frosting is creamy and fluffy, about 2 minutes more. Add any food coloring, if using, and beat on low speed until light and fluffy, about 30 seconds or until color is incorporated.

❹ Use immediately or store in an airtight container in the freezer for up to one month.

Icing Dos and Don'ts

To make the perfect icing, there are a few key tips to follow: Be sure not to overbeat when mixing; if you beat the icing more than 5 minutes it will become grainy. To get a pure white icing, use clear vanilla extract. To flavor your icing or include mix-ins, add them as you add the heavy cream. Beat until icing is creamy and fluffy.

The best part about my recipe is that a little less or more of any ingredient is okay. If your icing is too stiff, add a bit more cream, 2 tablespoons at a time, until it's to your liking. If it seems too thin, add more confectioners' sugar, 2 tablespoons at a time, until it reaches your desired consistency. It has a great shelf life, up to 1 month in the refrigerator and 3 months in the freezer. Be sure to allow ample time to thaw frozen icing, about 1 hour, before using.

This recipe can also be used as a simple glaze for dipping or drizzling over cookies. In a microwave-safe bowl, heat 1 cup of buttercream for 30 seconds on low power and stir. Add a tablespoon of milk and stir. Repeat if needed until the consistency is runny enough to drizzle over a cookie. To drizzle, tilt and wave your spoon back and forth about 6 inches (15 cm) above the cookie. To dip your cookie, carefully hold cookie by its edge and dunk into melted buttercream. Place on a cooling rack to dry.

BUTTERCREAM ICING MIX-INS

(amounts are for 1 standard batch of icing)

MAPLE EXTRACT: 1½ tablespoons

PUMPKIN SPICE EXTRACT: 1½ tablespoons

COCONUT EXTRACT: 1½ tablespoons

PEPPERMINT EXTRACT: 1½ tablespoons

ORANGE EXTRACT: 1½ tablespoons

INSTANT COFFEE: 3 tablespoons

COCOA POWDER: 1½ cups (150 g)

COOKIE CRUMBS: 1½ cups (150 g)

SPRINKLES: 1½ cups (350 g)

CINNAMON: 1½ tablespoons

JAM: ¼ cup (82 g)

LEMON EXTRACT: 1½ tablespoons

Decorating Cookies

Here comes the fun part! But first, some advice before beginning.

When decorating cookies, always use disposable pastry bags. They are faster and easier to use than a knife and much simpler to use with children, and they make cleanup a breeze. I prefer to use 12-inch (30.5-cm) bags. They hold less icing but allow me to keep a steadier hand while decorating.

Before attaching a decorating tip to your bag, consider using a coupler. Couplers make it easy to switch decorating tips without having to use a separate bag. Once your bag is ready to fill with icing, be sure to fill no more than half full to ensure a good grip and better control when piping. Overfilling your bag may result in a giant mess, with icing oozing out the top of the bag and giving your hand a cramp! The more icing you put inside the bag, the more icing your hand has to squeeze to pipe.

My number one decorating rule is to keep decorating simple. The more you add, the messier it can get. I typically keep faces and extra details to a minimum. Simplify decorating by using only two or three colors of icing. You'll save on cleanup time and still get gorgeous designs. You can also use one color and make three shades of it to give your cookies a gradient look.

When covering a cookie in icing, I always outline the cookie before filling it in. I prefer not to decorate all the way to the edges, leaving some of the cookie to show so that when it is transferred to a display piece or packaging, the cookie icing doesn't smear.

You only need a few decorating tips to create hundreds of designs. Each decorating tip is numbered, but different brands have

different numbering systems. I love to use Wilton decorating tips. A standard round decorating tip will likely be your new best friend. Wilton's #1 and #2 tips are great for writing and fine detail, while #3 and #4 tips are used more often for outlining and filling in shapes. Star tips (#16 and #18) are great for creating texture in cookies. I use them to make animal fur, snowflakes, types of food, and flowers. Flower designs in particular might require a bit more advanced decorating skills, but you don't need a lot of different kinds of tips to create pretty blossoms. For example, using the Wilton #104 tip can make several different designs; simply change the way you angle the bag and tip, from 45 degrees (see page 28) to vertically straight up and down and more.

The final piece of advice I can offer is this: When decorating cookies, do not stress about making your cookies look perfect! Give yourself a break and have fun with it. The more you decorate, the better you'll get. If you make a mistake, just scrape it off with a knife and start again—or better yet, eat it!

NOTE FROM JENNY

When snipping the tip of a pastry bag, don't cut off too much! It's always better to cut less and adjust or else your decorating tip or coupler may slide right out of the hole, especially when you exert pressure on the bag.

When to Break Out Couplers

Before you fill your pastry bag(s) with icing, decide how you plan to decorate. If you'll be using one color with just one tip, then snip the tip of the pastry bag, insert the decorating tip, fill the bag with icing, and get started! But if you want to use the same tip with more than one color, it's time to break out the couplers.

Couplers are a two-part plastic piece that allow you to change out tips on the same bag of icing. Snip the tip of the pastry bag, insert the coupler base so that it pokes out of the hole a bit, fit the desired tip on the base, and then screw on the coupler ring to hold the tip in place. When you want to change tips, simply unscrew the ring and repeat.

Sprinkles!

- *Sugar cookies become all the more whimsical with sprinkles, nonpareils, sanding sugars, and more. To make sure they stick, add them when the icing is not yet dry.*
- *Use sprinkles to disguise mistakes or messy decorating. Simply dip the decorated cookies into a bowl of sanding sugar or sprinkles and voilà!*
- *Add sprinkle accents to cookies by using them as elements on the cookie. Nonpareils become fans on a football field or the coat of a llama, brown sprinkles resemble Big Foot's fur, and a mixture of sprinkles stands in for candy. Get creative!*
- *Combine sanding sugar, nonpareils, confetti quinns, pearls, and sprinkles to create a personalized sprinkle mix.*

Packaging and Storing Cookies

The number one question I receive via email or social media is about how I package, store, and stack cookies. The buttercream icing on sugar cookies forms a crust on the top within about 6 to 8 hours. If necessary, you can spread the making, baking, and decorating process over several days or even longer with careful storage. Store decorated or undecorated cookies in an airtight container at room temperature for up to 4 days. Do not refrigerate as they will become soggy. The cookies freeze like a dream! Freeze fully decorated or undecorated cookies in an airtight container for up to 1 month. (I prefer to freeze them unfrosted, because decorated cookies will take up more space in your freezer.) Thaw at room temperature before serving or decorating (about 10 minutes).

When packaging, be sure to allow the cookies ample time to crust before packaging them in a bag or stacking in a box. Lay a piece of parchment paper between the layers of decorated cookies to avoid them sticking together. Use cupcake liners, parchment, or fabric to line the container before adding cookies. Finish with twine, ribbon, scraps of fabric, or a simple tag.

PACKAGING IDEAS

KRAFT PAPER TAKE-OUT BOX

CANNING JARS

WOODEN OR STURDY PAPER LOAF PAN

COOKIE TINS

VINTAGE CAKE, BREAD, AND PIE PANS

CELLOPHANE BAGS

VINTAGE BOXES

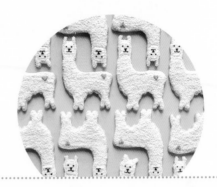

SPRING

A Sweet Snack

Old-Fashioned Donut

YOU WILL NEED

1 batch Sugar Cookie Dough (page 16)

Donut-shaped cookie cutter

2 pastry bags

2 Wilton #4 decorating tips

1 batch Buttercream Icing (page 26), divided and dyed into equal amounts of the following colors:

Pink

Dark brown

Rainbow sprinkles

Chocolate sprinkles

1½ cups cocoa powder (optional)

NOTES FROM JENNY

- *Try tasty options like chocolate- or maple-flavored buttercream icing!*
- *Deliver these donut cookies in a window donut box and it'll be hard to tell them apart from the real thing.*
- *Try coffee-flavored donut cookies frosted with espresso, chocolate, or pumpkin spice buttercream.*

❶ Follow baking instructions on page 16.

❷ Fit each pastry bag with a #4 decorating tip. Fill one with pink icing and the other with brown icing.

❸ Decorate half the cookies using the pink icing: Pipe a wavy line around the outer and inner edges of the cookie and fill with vertical lines. Sprinkle with rainbow sprinkles.

❹ Decorate the other half of the cookies using the brown icing: Pipe a wavy line around the outer and inner edges of the cookie and fill with vertical lines. Sprinkle with chocolate sprinkles.

Maple Bar

1 batch Sugar Cookie Dough
(page 16)

4-inch (10-cm) oblong cookie cutter

2 pastry bags

2 Wilton #4 decorating tips

1 batch Buttercream Icing (page 26),
divided and dyed into equal
amounts of the following colors:

  light brown

  dark brown

1½ tablespoons maple flavoring
(optional)

❶ Follow baking instructions on page 16.

❷ Fit each pastry bag with a #4 decorating tip. Fill one with light-brown icing and the other with dark-brown icing.

❸ Using the light-brown icing, outline the outer edge of the cookie and fill with horizontal lines.

❹ Using the dark-brown icing, pipe a squiggly line along the length of the cookie to resemble a chocolate drizzle.

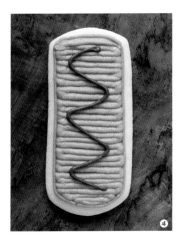

Spring Flowers

Daisy

YOU WILL NEED

1 batch Sugar Cookie Dough
(page 16)

1½-inch (3.81-cm) round cookie
cutter

2 pastry bags

1 Wilton #104 decorating tip

1 Wilton #4 decorating tip

1 batch Buttercream Icing (page
26), divided and dyed as follows:

    ½ cup (120 ml) golden yellow

    remainder undyed (white)

NOTE FROM JENNY
*Serve these cookies on a vintage
tray for a spring lunch or pair with
bunny and carrot cookies for a spring
garden theme.*

❶ Follow baking instructions on
page 16.

❷ Fit one pastry bag with the
#104 decorating tip and
fill with white icing. Fit one
pastry bag with the #4
decorating tip and fill with
golden-yellow icing.

❸ Using the white icing and
starting about ½ inch (12
mm) from the outer edge,
pipe a petal onto the cookie,
holding the bag, with the
larger side of the tip up, at a
45-degree angle, squeezing
then releasing pressure as you
pull to the center. Repeat the
petals around the outer edge.

❹ Using the golden-yellow icing
and holding the bag vertically,
dot a circle to create the
center of the daisy.

Hydrangea

1 batch Sugar Cookie Dough (page 16)

2½-inch (6.35-cm) round cookie cutter

3 pastry bags

1 Wilton #352 decorating tip

2 Wilton #2D decorating tips

1 batch Buttercream Icing (page 26), divided and dyed as follows:

    ½ cup (120 ml) green

    2 cups (480 ml) soft pink

    2 cups (480 ml) soft blue

    remainder undyed (white)

❶ Follow baking instructions on page 16.

❷ Fit one pastry bag with the #352 decorating tip and fill with green icing. Fit one pastry bag with the #2D decorating tip. Fill the bag on one side with soft-pink icing and the other side with white icing. This will give the icing a two-toned effect. Fit one pastry bag with the #2D decorating tip, and fill the bag on one side with soft-blue icing and the other side with white icing.

❸ Using the green icing and starting about ¼ inch (6 mm) from the outer edge, pipe two or three leaves onto a cookie, holding the bag at a 45-degree angle. The two points of the tip should resemble a bird's vertical open beak. Squeeze to form the base of the leaf and then release pressure to form a leaf point. Repeat with the remaining cookies.

❹ Using the soft-blue and white icing bag, hold the bag vertically and pipe four or five petals onto the top of a cookie. Move toward the center of the cookie and make another layer of petals over the first layer. Complete the cookie by adding a few petals in the center. Repeat with half of the cookies.

❺ Using the soft-pink and white icing bag, repeat step 4 on the remaining half of the cookies.

Llamas

1 batch Sugar Cookie Dough
(page 16)

Llama-shaped cookie cutter

3 pastry bags

1 #4 Wilton decorating tip

1 #2 Wilton decorating tip

1 #3 Wilton decorating tip

1 batch Buttercream Icing (page
26), divided and dyed as follows:

　¾ cup (180 ml) black

　¾ cup (180 ml) pink

　remainder undyed (white)

White nonpareils or sprinkles

NOTES FROM JENNY

▶ *You can make these cookies look
lifelike by dipping them in white
sprinkles after decorating them
with icing.*

▶ *To make fluffy buttercream fur,
instead of sprinkles use a #18
or #223 decorating tip to fill in
each llama's body with textured
buttercream.*

❶ Follow baking instructions on
page 16.

❷ Fit one pastry bag with the
#4 decorating tip and fill with
white icing. Fit one pastry
bag with the #2 decorating
tip and fill with black icing.
Fit one pastry bag with the
#3 decorating tip and fill with
pink icing.

❸ Using the white icing, pipe an
outline around the outer edge
of the cookie, and fill the body
with curved horizontal lines.
Dip the iced cookie in white
nonpareils or sprinkles. Fill in
the face with white icing.

❹ Using the pink icing, pipe a
small heart on the llama's
backside.

❺ Using the black icing, pipe the
llama's face.

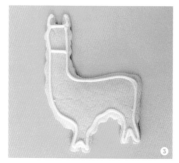

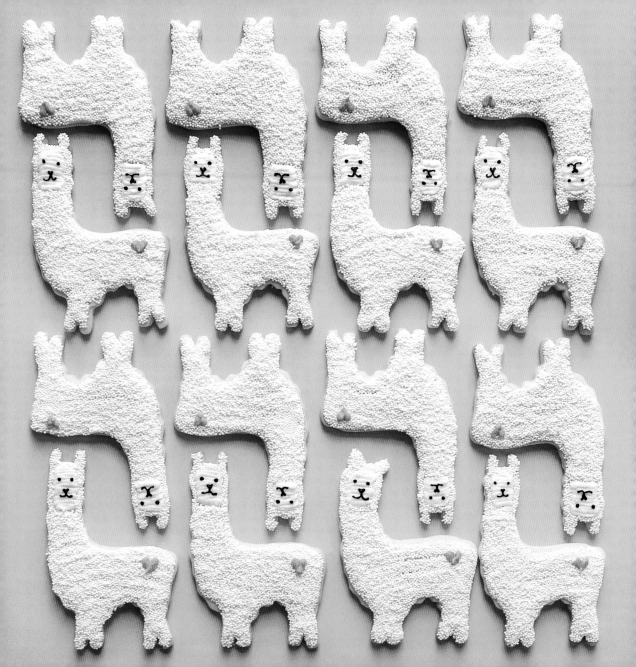

A Box of Chocolates

1 batch Sugar Cookie Dough (page 16) using cocoa powder mix-in (page 23)

1-inch (2.5-cm) round cookie cutter

1-inch (2.5-cm) square cookie cutter

1½-inch (3.81-cm) long rectangular cookie cutter

5 pastry bags

2 Wilton #5 decorating tips

2 Wilton #1A decorating tips

1 Wilton #1 decorating tip

1 batch Buttercream Icing (page 26), divided and dyed as follows:

   ½ cup (120 ml) undyed (white)

   Half remaining light brown

   Half remaining dark brown

Coarse clear sanding sugar

Chocolate sprinkles

NOTE FROM JENNY
If you don't like chocolate, you can bake the shapes using basic cookie dough and color the icing in shades of brown.

❶ Follow baking instructions on page 16. Cut out a variety of shapes using the round, square, and rectangular cutters.

❷ Fit two pastry bags with the #5 decorating tips. Fill one with light-brown icing and the other with dark-brown icing. Fit two pastry bags with the #1A decorating tips. Fill one with light-brown icing and the other with dark-brown icing. Fit one pastry bag with the #1 decorating tip and fill with white icing.

❸ Using the bags fitted with the #1A decorating tips, cover the tops of the round cookies, making half of the cookies light brown and the other half dark brown. Sprinkle some with chocolate sprinkles, some with clear sanding sugar, and leave some without any sprinkles.

❹ Using the bags fitted with the #5 decorating tips, pipe an outline on the square cookies, then fill with vertical lines, making half of the cookies light brown and the other half dark brown. Using the bag fitted with the #1 tip, pipe a drizzle of lines onto the tops of some of the cookies, and sprinkle others with chocolate sprinkles or sanding sugar.

❺ Using the bags fitted with the #5 decorating tips, pipe a simple line on the rectangle cookies to cover. Using the bag fitted with the #1 decorating tip, pipe a drizzle of lines onto the tops of some of the cookies.

Swans

YOU WILL NEED

1 batch Sugar Cookie Dough (page 16)

Swan-shaped cookie cutter

4 pastry bags

1 Wilton #10 decorating tip

1 Wilton #352 decorating tip

1 Wilton #3 decorating tip

1 Wilton #2 decorating tip

1 batch Buttercream Icing (page 26), divided and dyed as follows:

   ½ cup (120 ml) pink

   ½ cup (120 ml) black

   remainder undyed (white)

NOTE FROM JENNY

Flip some of the cut-out swans upside down before baking so the cookie swans can face each other when displayed.

❶ Follow baking instructions on page 16.

❷ Fit one pastry bag with the #10 decorating tip and another with the #352 decorating tip, and fill both with white icing.

Fit one pastry bag with the #3 decorating tip and fill with pink icing. Fit one pastry bag with the #2 decorating tip and fill with black icing.

❸ Using the bag with the #10 decorating tip, and beginning at the top of the swan's head, pipe down the neck (use enough pressure along the neck to fill the area) then outline the swan's body.

❹ Using the bag with the #352 decorating tip, and beginning at the swan's tail, pipe a feather onto the cookie, holding the bag at a 45-degree angle. The two points of the tip should resemble a bird's open beak. Squeeze then release pressure while lifting up to create a "feather." Repeat in horizontal rows to fill the swan's body.

❺ Using the pink icing, pipe the swan's beak. Using the black icing, pipe the swan's eye.

St. Patrick's Day

Shamrock

YOU WILL NEED

½ batch Sugar Cookie Dough (page 16)

Clover-shaped cookie cutter

1 pastry bag

1 Wilton #4 decorating tip

½ batch Buttercream Icing (page 26), dyed green

Clear sanding sugar

NOTE FROM JENNY

Try serving these with lime sherbet punch or sparkling cucumber limeade (or even green beer if you prefer) for a special treat on St. Paddy's Day!

❶ Follow baking instructions on page 16.

❷ Fit the pastry bag with the #4 decorating tip and fill with green icing.

❸ Pipe the outline of a shamrock using the shape of the cookie as a guide, then fill in each lobe of the shamrock leaf with a back-and-forth motion, turning the cookie so each lobe is filled with horizontal lines. Add a stem at the bottom.

❹ Dip the iced cookie in sanding sugar.

Rainbow

½ batch Sugar Cookie Dough (page 16)

Rainbow-shaped cookie cutter

9 pastry bags

1 Wilton #18 decorating tip

8 Wilton #4 decorating tips

½ batch Buttercream Icing (page 26), divided and dyed into equal amounts of the following colors:

Red, Pink, Orange, Yellow, Green, Blue, Purple, Brown, Undyed (white)

White sanding sugar

Gold sanding sugar

Gold nonpareils

1. Follow baking instructions on page 16.

2. Fit one pastry bag with the #18 decorating tip and fill with white icing. Fit eight pastry bags with the #4 decorating tips and fill each with the remaining colors of icing.

3. Using the red icing, pipe a row along the outer edge of the cookies with a tight zigzag, sparing the cloud and the pot of gold. Continue making successive rows using the pink, orange, yellow, green, blue, and purple icings, always sparing the cloud and the pot of gold.

4. Using the bag with the #18 decorating tip, create a billowy cloud using a swirling motion to fill the space. Pipe a line across the bottom of the other side of the rainbow, which will become the gold in the pot.

5. Using the brown icing, pipe an outline around the outer edge of the pot of gold, and fill in the area with horizontal lines. Sprinkle gold nonpareils and gold sanding sugar on the top edge of the pot to resemble gold sitting in it.

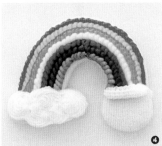

Bunnies

YOU WILL NEED

1 batch Sugar Cookie Dough (page 16)

Rabbit-shaped cookie cutter

3 pastry bags

2 couplers

2 Wilton #4 decorating tips

2 Wilton #18 decorating tips

1 batch Buttercream Icing (page 26), divided and dyed as follows:

    ½ cup (120 ml) pink

    half remaining undyed (white)

    half remaining brown or chocolate

Brown sprinkles

White sprinkles

1½ cups cocoa powder (optional)

NOTES FROM JENNY

- *Divide the icing and mix half with cocoa powder for chocolate and classic vanilla buttercream options.*
- *Dip these cookies in sprinkles for a textured bunny coat and complete with a fluffy rosette tail.*

❶ Follow baking instructions on page 16.

❷ Fit one pastry bag with the #4 decorating tip and fill with white icing. Fit one pastry bag with a coupler and the #4 decorating tip and fill with brown icing. Fit one pastry bag with a coupler and the #18 decorating tip and fill with pink icing.

❸ Using the white icing, pipe an outline around the outer edge of half of the cookies, and fill with horizontal lines. Dip the iced cookies in white sprinkles.

❹ Using the brown icing, pipe an outline around the outer edge of the remaining cookies and fill with horizontal lines. Dip the iced cookies in brown sprinkles.

❺ Using the pink icing, pipe puffy rosette tails on the white icing bunnies.

❻ Switch the decorating tip on the white icing to the #18 decorating tip. Use this icing to pipe fluffy rosette tails on the brown icing bunnies.

Cinco de Mayo

Cactus

1 batch Sugar Cookie Dough (page 16)

Cactus-shaped cookie cutter

1 pastry bag

1 Wilton #199 decorating tip

1 batch Buttercream Icing (page 26), dyed green

White sprinkles

❶ Follow baking instructions on page 16.

❷ Fit the pastry bag with the #199 decorating tip and fill with green icing. Pipe a line down each arm of the cactus. Repeat down the center of the cactus.

❸ Sprinkle lightly with white sprinkles.

Piñata

1 batch Sugar Cookie Dough (page 16)

Donkey-shaped cookie cutter

5 pastry bags

5 Wilton #4 decorating tips

1 batch Buttercream Icing (page 26), divided and dyed into equal amounts of the following colors: Pink, Orange, Red , Yellow, Green

❶ Follow baking instructions on page 16.

❷ Fit the pastry bags with the #4 decorating tips and fill each of the bags with one color of icing.

❸ Starting at the top of the donkey, pipe tight zigzag rows of each color, starting with pink and following with orange, red, yellow, and green, repeating the sequence until the piñata is completely covered.

Breakfast of Champions

Coffee Cup

YOU WILL NEED

1 batch Sugar Cookie Dough (page 16)

Mug-shaped cookie cutter

2 pastry bags

2 Wilton #4 decorating tips

1 batch Buttercream Icing (page 26), divided and dyed as follows:

    1 cup (240 ml) dark brown

    remainder undyed (white)

NOTE FROM JENNY

Try adding instant coffee to the brown icing on the coffee cups to enhance the flavor of these cookies.

❶ Follow baking instructions on page 16.

❷ Fit the pastry bags with the #4 decorating tips. Fill one with brown icing and the other with white icing.

❸ Using the white icing, pipe the outline of a mug, excluding the handle but adding a narrow oval along the top edge of the cup for the "coffee."

❹ Using the white icing, make horizontal lines to fill in the coffee mug. Pipe a thick semicircle to create the mug handle. Using the brown icing, fill in the oval.

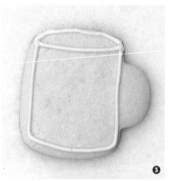

BREAKFAST IN BED

- [x] bacon
- [x] avocado toast
- [x] over easy eggs
- [x] fresh fruit
- [x] black coffee
- [x] orange juice

Avocado Toast

1 batch Sugar Cookie Dough (page 16)

Toast-shaped cookie cutter

2 pastry bags

1 Wilton #4 decorating tip

1 Wilton #1A decorating tip

1 batch Buttercream Icing (page 26), divided and dyed as follows:

   1 cup (240 ml) light brown

   remainder avocado green

Black sanding sugar

Clear sanding sugar

❶ Follow baking instructions on page 16.

❷ Fit one pastry bag with the #4 decorating tip and fill with light-brown icing. Fit one pastry bag with the #1A decorating tip and fill with green icing.

❸ Using the light-brown icing, pipe an outline around the outer edge of the cookie to resemble the toasted edge.

❹ Using the avocado-green icing, fill the outlined area with horizontal lines.

❺ Using a small spoon or offset spatula, "mess up" the icing to resemble mashed avocado. Sprinkle with black and clear sanding sugar.

❸

❹

❺

Bacon

1 batch Sugar Cookie Dough
(page 16)

Bacon-shaped cookie cutter

1 pastry bag

1 Wilton #113 decorating tip

1 batch Buttercream Icing (page 26),
divided and dyed as follows:

    ½ cup (120 ml) dark brown

    remainder light brown

❶ Follow baking instructions on
page 16.

❷ Fit the pastry bag with the
#113 decorating tip. Smear
a small amount of dark-
brown icing down one side of
the pastry bag, then fill the
remainder of the bag with
light-brown icing. This will give
the icing a two-toned effect.

❸ Starting at one end of the
cookie, pipe icing from one
end to the other, holding the
tip at an angle and rippling
the icing slightly as you go to
resemble a strip of bacon.

❷

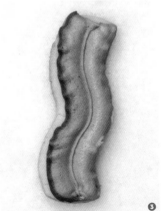

❸

Sunny-Side-Up Eggs

1 batch Sugar Cookie Dough
(page 16)

2½-inch (6.35-cm) oval cookie
cutter

2 pastry bags

1 Wilton #4 decorating tip

1 Wilton #1A decorating tip

1 batch Buttercream Icing (page 26),
divided and dyed as follows:

  two-thirds undyed (white)

  one-third golden yellow

❶ Follow baking instructions on
page 16.

❷ Fit one pastry bag with the
#4 decorating tip and fill with
white icing. Fit one pastry
bag with the #1A decorating
tip and fill with golden-yellow
icing.

❸ Using the white icing, pipe
an outline to resemble two
joined circles (like the outside
of the number 8) and fill with
vertical lines.

❹ Using the golden-yellow icing,
and holding the bag vertically,
squeeze two large dollops of
icing to resemble the yolks of
sunny-side-up eggs.

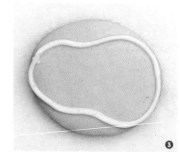

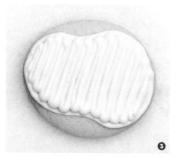

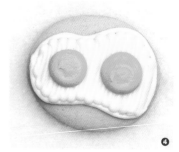

Buttered Toast

1 batch Sugar Cookie Dough
(page 16)

Toast-shaped cookie cutter

2 pastry bags

2 Wilton #4 decorating tips

1 batch Buttercream Icing (page 26),
divided and dyed as follows:

  1 cup (240 ml) yellow

  two-thirds remaining ivory

  one-third remaining light brown

❶ Follow baking instructions on
page 16.

❷ Place the yellow icing in the
middle of a piece of plastic
wrap and form into a squared-
off log to resemble a stick
of butter. Wrap snugly and
freeze for an hour. Once fully
hard, carefully slice "butter
pats" and store in fridge.

❸ Fit the pastry bags with the
#4 decorating tips. Fill one
with ivory icing and the other
with light-brown icing.

❹ Using the light-brown icing,
pipe an outline around the
outer edge of the cookie to
resemble the toasted edge.
Using the ivory icing, fill the
outlined area with horizontal
lines.

❺ Place two "butter pats" in the
center.

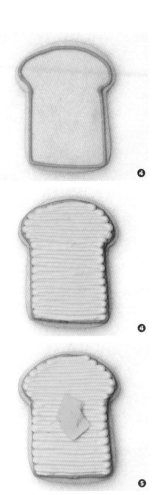

Flowers for Mom

Ribbon Rose

YOU WILL NEED

1 batch Sugar Cookie Dough (page 16)

2½-inch (6.35-cm) round cookie cutter

2 pastry bags

1 Wilton #4 decorating tip

1 Wilton #104 decorating tip

1 batch Buttercream Icing (page 26), divided and dyed as follows:

one-third undyed (white)

two-thirds peach

❶ Follow baking instructions on page 16.

❷ Fit one pastry bag with the #4 decorating tip and fill with white icing. Fit one pastry bag with the #104 decorating tip and fill with peach icing.

❸ Using the white icing, pipe a small mound in the center of a cookie. Holding your bag vertically, pipe small dots onto the mound to create a flower center.

❹ Using the peach icing and holding the bag horizontally with the large end of the tip down, pipe a continuous petal around the center mound, rotating the cookie with your opposite hand (or on a turntable) until you reach the outer edge of the cookie.

NOTE FROM JENNY
These buttercream flowers can be created year-round by choosing icing colors to coordinate with the season.

Anemone

1 batch Sugar Cookie Dough
(page 16)

2½-inch (6.35-cm) round cookie
cutter

2 pastry bags

1 Wilton #104 decorating tip

1 Wilton #4 decorating tip

1 batch Buttercream Icing (page 26),
divided and dyed as follows:

   ½ cup (120 ml) black

   remainder undyed (white)

❶ Follow baking instructions on
page 16.

❷ Fit one pastry bag with the
#104 decorating tip and
fill with white icing. Fit one
pastry bag with the #4
decorating tip and fill with
black icing.

❸ Using the white icing and
starting about ½ inch (12
mm) from outer edge, pipe
individual petals around the
entire edge, holding the bag at
a 45-degree angle while using
small back-and-forth motions
to create a ruffled look.

❹ Move toward the center of the
cookie and make a second
and third layer of petals.

❺ Using the black icing, pipe
a dollop in the center, then
pipe small vertical black lines
around the dollop.

Ranunculus

1 batch Sugar Cookie Dough (page 16)

2½-inch (6.35-cm) round cookie cutter

3 pastry bags

3 Wilton #104 decorating tips

1 batch Buttercream Icing (page 26), divided and dyed into equal amounts of the following colors:

    undyed (white)

    light peach

    peach

❶ Follow baking instructions on page 16.

❷ Fit the pastry bags with the #104 decorating tips and fill with each of the colors of icing.

❸ Using the white icing, starting at the center of a cookie, pipe a small mound. Holding your tip at the base of the mound, pipe petals over the top of the mound. Rotate the cookie to make overlapping petals until the white icing mound is covered. It should resemble the closed inner petals of a rose.

❹ Using the light-peach icing, continue to pipe overlapping petals around the cookie until about ½ inch (12 mm) from the edge.

❺ Using the peach icing, continue to pipe overlapping petals around the cookie until you reach the edge.

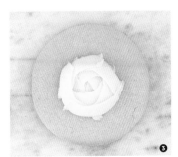

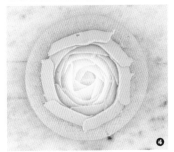

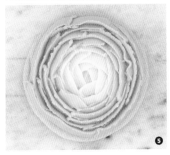

Zinnia

1 batch Sugar Cookie Dough
(page 16)

2½-inch (6.35-cm) round cookie
cutter

2 pastry bags

1 Wilton #104 decorating tip

1 Wilton #4 decorating tip

1 batch Buttercream Icing (page 26),
divided and dyed as follows:

    ½ cup (120 ml) undyed (white)

    remainder peach

❶ Follow baking instructions on
page 16.

❷ Fit one pastry bag with the
#104 decorating tip and
fill with peach icing. Fit
one pastry bag with the #4
decorating tip and fill with
white icing.

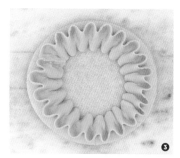

❸ Using the peach icing and
starting from the outer
edge of the cookie, pipe a
continuous petal while using
short up-and-down motions
to create a ruffled look,
rotating the cookie with the
opposite hand.

❹ Move toward the center of
the cookie and make another
layer of continuous petals
over the first layer.

❺ Pipe a third layer of petals.

❻ Using the white icing, pipe
three small dots at the center
of the flower.

Take Me Out to the Ball Game

Baseball

NOTE FROM JENNY

Serve with a side of Cracker Jack!

❶ Follow baking instructions on page 16.

❷ Fit one pastry bag with the #4 decorating tip and fill with white icing. Fit one pastry bag with the #3 decorating tip and fill with red icing.

❸ Using the white icing, pipe an outline around the outer edge of the cookie and fill with horizontal lines.

❹ Using the red icing, pipe lines with little Vs on the baseball to resemble stitching.

Baseball Glove

1 batch Sugar Cookie Dough
(page 16)

Baseball glove–shaped cookie
cutter

2 pastry bags

1 Wilton #4 decorating tip

1 Wilton #3 decorating tip

1 batch Buttercream Icing (page 26),
divided and dyed as follows:

    1 cup (240 ml) undyed (white)

    remainder brown

❶ Follow baking instructions on
page 16.

❷ Fit one pastry bag with the
#4 decorating tip and fill with
brown icing. Fit one pastry
bag with the #3 decorating tip
and fill with white icing.

❸ Using the brown icing, pipe
an outline around the outer
edge of the cookie and
fill with horizontal lines,
completing each finger of the
glove separately.

❹ Using the white icing, pipe
lines on the glove to resemble
stitching.

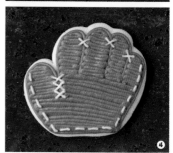

Baseball Bat

YOU WILL NEED

1 batch Sugar Cookie Dough
(page 16)

Baseball bat–shaped cookie cutter

2 pastry bags

1 Wilton #4 decorating tip

1 Wilton #3 decorating tip

1 batch Buttercream Icing (page 26),
divided and dyed as follows:

    ½ cup (120 ml) undyed (white)

    remainder brown

❶ Follow baking instructions on
page 16.

❷ Fit one pastry bag with the
#4 decorating tip and fill with
brown icing. Fit one pastry
bag with the #3 decorating tip
and fill with white icing.

❸ Using the brown icing, pipe
an outline around the cookie
and fill with zigzag lines.

❹ Using the white icing, pipe two
lines at the bottom of the bat.

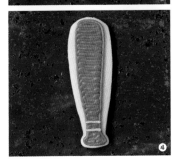

Baseball Jersey

YOU WILL NEED

1 batch Sugar Cookie Dough (page 16)

V-neck T-shirt–shaped cookie cutter

2 pastry bags

1 Wilton #4 decorating tip

1 Wilton #2 decorating tip

1 batch Buttercream Icing (page 26), divided and dyed as follows:

   1 cup (240 ml) undyed (white)

   remainder red

NOTE FROM JENNY

Personalize jerseys with player numbers or decorate in your favorite team's colors.

❶ Follow baking instructions on page 16.

❷ Fit one pastry bag with the #4 decorating tip and fill with red icing. Fit one pastry bag with the #2 decorating tip and fill with white icing.

❸ Using the white icing, pipe an outline around the outer edge of the cookie and fill with horizontal lines. Pipe a line down the center of the cookie and a few dots alongside the line, creating the look of a button-down jersey as shown in the photo on page 71.

❹ Using the white icing, pipe lines at the edges of the sleeves and two vertical lines down the front to create the appearance of a jersey.

Hearts and Diamonds

Floral Heart

YOU WILL NEED

1 batch Sugar Cookie Dough
(page 16)

Heart-shaped cookie cutter

4 pastry bags

1 Wilton #4 decorating tip

1 Wilton #16 decorating tip

1 Wilton #18 decorating tip

1 Wilton #80 decorating tip

1 batch Buttercream Icing (page
26), divided and dyed as follows:

   ½ cup (120 ml) dark green

   1 cup (240 ml) light green

   ½ (cup 120 ml) pink icing

   remainder light pink

❶ Follow baking instructions on
page 16.

❷ Fit one pastry bag with the
#4 decorating tip and fill with
light-pink icing. Fit one pastry
bag with the #16 decorating
tip and fill with pink icing. Fit
one pastry bag with the #80
decorating tip and fill with
light-green icing. Fit one pastry
bag with the #18 tip and fill
with dark-green icing.

❸ Using the light-pink icing, pipe
an outline around the outer
edge of the cookie and fill with
horizontal lines.

❹ Using the light-green icing, pipe
a small succulent onto the
cookie. Begin by piping small,
individual petals in a circle in
the top left corner of the heart.
Pipe another layer of petals
over the first layer. Finish with a
few petals in the center.

❺ Using the pink icing, pipe two rosettes on either side of the
succulent.

❻ Using the dark-green icing and holding the bag vertically, pipe a
few stars alongside the rosettes and succulent. Using the pink
icing, pipe smaller stars among the dark-green stars.

Diamond Ring

1 batch Sugar Cookie Dough
(page 16)

Diamond ring–shaped cookie cutter

7 pastry bags

1 Wilton #4 decorating tip

1 Wilton #10 decorating tip

1 Wilton #16 decorating tip

3 Wilton #18 decorating tips

1 Wilton #80 decorating tip

1 batch Buttercream Icing (page
26), divided and dyed as follows:

½ cup (120 ml) light green

½ cup (120 ml) light pink

½ cup (120 ml) pink

½ cup (120 ml) dark green

2 cups (480 ml) gray

remainder undyed (white)

Clear edible glitter

NOTE FROM JENNY

*Match the icing colors on the hearts with
your party colors or personalize with the
couple's initials or wedding date.*

❶ Follow baking instructions on page 16.

❷ Fit one pastry bag with the #4 decorating tip and fill with white icing. Fit one pastry bag with the #10 decorating tip and fill with gray icing. Fit one pastry bag with the #16 decorating tip and fill with pink icing. Fit one pastry bag with the #80 decorating tip and fill with light-green icing. Fit three pastry bags with #18 tips and fill with light-pink, pink, and dark-green icing.

❸ Using the white icing, outline the shape of a diamond at the top of the cookie, keeping ¼ inch (6 mm) from the edge, and fill with horizontal lines. Pipe the lines of the facets as shown in the photo. Sprinkle the diamond with edible glitter to make it sparkle.

❹ Using the gray icing, pipe a line on each side of the diamond to resemble prongs. Starting from the base of the diamond and applying more pressure, pipe a line that follows the edge of the cookie to create a ring.

❺ Using the light-pink icing, pipe two rosettes at the lower right base of the ring.

❻ Using the dark-green icing and holding the bag vertically, pipe five stars next to the rosettes.

❼ Using the pink icing, pipe five small stars among the dark-green stars, as shown in the photo.

❽ Using the light-green icing, fill in the empty spaces among the stars with small leaves.

A Succulent Garden

Aloe Vera

1 batch Sugar Cookie Dough (page 16)

2½-inch (6.35-cm) round cookie cutter

1 pastry bag

1 Wilton #199 decorating tip

1 batch Buttercream Icing (page 26), dyed green

NOTE FROM JENNY

Swap the bright-pink icing for a deep plum and pair with pumpkin cookies in the fall, or use soft pink for a succulent-themed spring bridal or baby shower.

❶ Follow baking instructions on page 16.

❷ Fit the pastry bag with the #199 decorating tip and fill with green icing.

❸ Starting ½ inch (12 mm) from the outer edge of the cookie, pipe individual petals around the entire edge, pulling the icing toward the outer edge of the cookie.

❹ Move toward the center of the cookie and pipe another layer of petals over the first layer.

❺ Finish with a few petals in the center.

Echeveria

1 batch Sugar Cookie Dough (page 16)

2½-inch (6.35-cm) round cookie cutter

1 pastry bag

1 Wilton #352 decorating tip

1 batch Buttercream Icing (page 26), divided and dyed into equal amounts of the following colors:

> green
>
> bright pink

❶ Follow baking instructions on page 16.

❷ Fit the pastry bag with the #352 decorating tip and fill the bag on one side with green icing and the other half with bright-pink icing. This will give the icing a two-toned effect.

❸ Starting ½ inch (12 mm) from the outer edge of the cookie, pipe individual petals around the entire edge. The two points of the tip should resemble a bird's vertical open beak. Squeeze to form the base of each leaf and gently release pressure to form each point, pulling the icing toward the outer edge of the cookie. Repeat individual petals around the entire edge.

❹ Move toward the center of the cookie and pipe another layer of petals over the first layer.

❺ Finish with a few petals in the center.

Agave

YOU WILL NEED

1 batch Sugar Cookie Dough (page 16)

2½-inch (6.35-cm) round cookie cutter

1 pastry bag

1 Wilton #366 decorating tip

1 batch Buttercream Icing (page 26), dyed light green

❶ Follow baking instructions on page 16.

❷ Fit the pastry bag with the #366 decorating tip and fill with light-green icing.

❸ Starting ½ inch (12 mm) from the outer edge of the cookie, pipe individual petals around the entire edge. The two points of the tip should resemble a bird's vertical open beak. Squeeze to form the base of each leaf and then gently release pressure to form each point, pulling the icing toward the outer edge of the cookie. Repeat individual petals around the entire edge.

❹ Move toward the center of the cookie and pipe another layer of petals over the first layer.

❺ Finish with a few petals in the center.

Cactus Garden

1 batch Sugar Cookie Dough
(page 16)

2½-inch (6.35-cm) round cookie
cutter

2 pastry bags

1 Wilton #199 decorating tip

1 Wilton #16 decorating tip

1 batch Buttercream Icing (page 26),
divided and dyed as follows:

  1 cup (240 ml) pink

  remainder green

❶ Follow baking instructions on page 16.

❷ Fit one pastry bag with the #199 decorating tip and fill with green icing. Fit one pastry bag with the #16 decorating tip and fill with pink icing.

❸ Using the green icing and holding the bag vertically, pipe a few cacti, squeezing and releasing for each one and using a sizeable amount of icing each time. Repeat with less pressure to create a few smaller cacti. Fill the surface of the cookie with the cacti.

❹ Using the pink icing and holding the bag vertically, pipe small, random pink flowers onto the tips of some of the cacti.

Desert Rose

1 batch Sugar Cookie Dough (page 16)

2½-inch (6.35-cm) round cookie cutter

1 pastry bag

1 Wilton #104 decorating tip

1 batch Buttercream Icing (page 26), dyed bright pink

❶ Follow baking instructions on page 16.

❷ Fit the pastry bag with the #104 decorating tip and fill with the bright-pink icing.

❸ Starting at the center of the cookie, pipe a small mound. Holding your tip at the base of the mound, pipe petals over the top of the mound. Rotate the cookie to make overlapping petals until the icing mound is covered. It should resemble the closed inner petals of a rose.

❹ Continue to pipe overlapping petals until you reach the edge of the cookie.

SUMMER

Popsicles

1 batch Sugar Cookie Dough (page 16)

Popsicle-shaped cookie cutter

4 pastry bags

4 Wilton #4 decorating tips

1 batch Buttercream Icing (page 26), divided equally and dyed into four gradient shades of dusty blue

---

NOTE FROM JENNY

Think outside the box by adding a coordinating flavor to icing colors. Orange-flavored icing and coloring would make for a fun Creamsicle treat.

❶ Follow baking instructions on page 16.

❷ Fit the pastry bags with the #4 decorating tips and fill them with the gradient shades of dusty-blue icing.

❸ Using one color of icing, pipe an outline around the outer edge of one-quarter of the cookies, sparing the "stick," and fill in with horizontal lines. Repeat with the remaining colors.

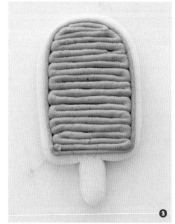

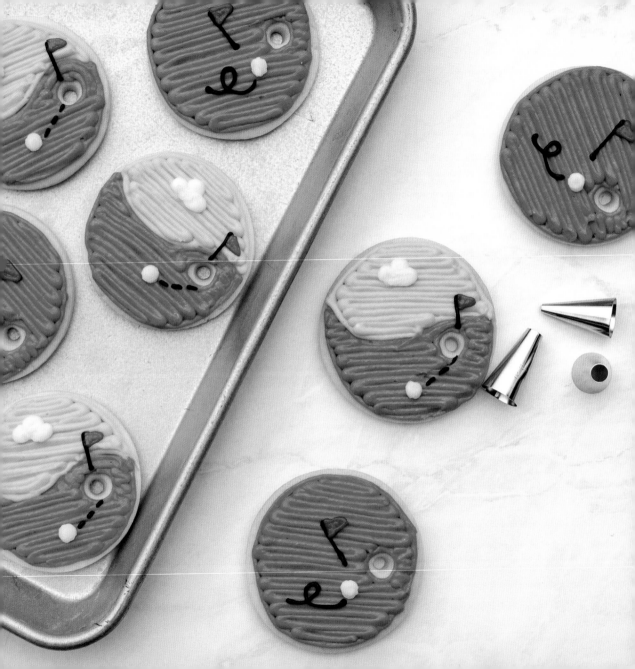

Hole in One

YOU WILL NEED

1 batch Sugar Cookie Dough
(page 16)

2½-inch (6.35-cm) round cookie
cutter

5 pastry bags

1 Wilton #10 decorating tip

5 Wilton #4 decorating tips

1 batch Buttercream Icing (page 26),
divided and dyed as follows:

　1 cup (240 ml) red

　1 cup (240 ml) undyed (white)

　1 cup (240 ml) black

　Half remaining light blue

　Half remaining light green

NOTE FROM JENNY
*These cookies are perfect for the golf
enthusiast—or a hole-in-one Father's
Day treat!*

❶ Cut the sugar cookie dough using the cookie cutter, then use the #10 decorating tip to remove a hole. Bake according to the directions on page 16. Let the cookies cool completely.

❷ Fit the pastry bags with the #4 decorating tips and fill with each icing color.

❸ On some cookies, using the light-green icing, pipe an outline around the outer edge and around the hole, then fill with horizontal lines.

❹ Using the black icing, pipe a line with a loop or a dashed line to resemble the golf ball's path toward the hole, and pipe a line for the flagpole. Using the red icing, pipe a triangular flag at the top of the pole. Using the white icing, pipe a dot for the golf ball at the end of the line.

❺ On the remainder of the cookies, using the light-blue icing, pipe a curved line across the bottom third of the cookie (above the hole) and then outline along the top of the cookie; this will be the sky. Fill with horizontal lines. Using the light-green icing, pipe along the curved line and the bottom of the cookie plus around the hole, then fill with horizontal lines.

❻ Repeat step 4 to further decorate the cookies.

❼ Using the white icing, pipe a puffy cloud in the sky on some cookies.

Sprinkle Sandwich Cookies

1 batch Sugar Cookie Dough (page 16)

1½ cups (240 g) sprinkles

2-inch (5-cm) round cookie cutter

1 batch Buttercream Icing (page 26), undyed (white)

NOTES FROM JENNY

▶ *Toss your favorite sprinkle colors into the batter, fill with rainbow sprinkle–filled icing, and roll completed cookie in coordinating sprinkles.*

▶ *Package a stack of these sandwich cookies in a tall cellophane bag with a coordinating ribbon for easy party favors!*

▶ *For a fun variation, cut the dough into hearts or stars. Try filling your sandwich cookies with your favorite ice cream instead of icing!*

❶ Mix ½ cup (80 g) of the sprinkles into the cookie dough until fully incorporated.

❷ Cut the dough using the cookie cutter and bake according to the directions on page 16. Let the cookies cool completely.

❸ Place a generous dollop of the icing on the back of one cookie, then top with another cookie. Repeat for the remaining cookies.

❹ Place the remaining 1 cup (160 g) of the sprinkles in a shallow bowl. Roll the edges of the cookies in the sprinkles to coat.

Under the Sea

Mermaid Tail

1 batch Sugar Cookie Dough
(page 16)

Mermaid tail–shaped cookie cutter

2 pastry bags

1 Wilton #104 decorating tip

1 Wilton #4 decorating tip

1 batch Buttercream Icing (page 26),
divided and dyed into equal amounts
of the following colors:

  purple

  turquoise

NOTE FROM JENNY

*Serve on a tray of brown sugar for a
sandy backdrop or package individually
in a small cookie box or cellophane bag
tied with a coordinating twine for a
mermaid-themed birthday party.*

❶ Follow baking instructions on
page 16.

❷ Fit one pastry bag with the
#104 decorating tip and
fill with purple icing. Fit
one pastry bag with the #4
decorating tip and fill with
turquoise icing.

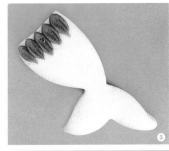

❸ Using the purple icing and
starting at the wide end of the
tail, squeeze while dragging the
tip toward the fins, then release
to make a fish scale. Continue
across the top to create a row of
scales. Make more rows toward
the end of the tail, overlapping
each previous row slightly, until
completely covered.

❹ Using the turquoise icing, pipe
an outline around the fins
and fill with lines to match the
curve of the tail.

Clamshell

1 batch Sugar Cookie Dough
(page 16)

Clamshell-shaped cookie cutter

1 pastry bag

1 Wilton #10 decorating tip

1 batch Buttercream Icing (page 26),
dyed purple

White nonpareils

Edible glitter

White Sixlets candies

Blue sprinkles

❶ Follow baking instructions on
page 16.

❷ Fit the pastry bag with the
#10 tip and fill with purple
icing.

❸ Starting at the top middle
of the clamshell, pipe a line
of icing toward the bottom,
stopping before the edge.
Continue piping lines,
overlapping the previous
row slightly, until completely
covered.

❹ Rotate the cookie 180
degrees and pipe a row
of short overlapping lines
coming from the other side.

❺ Sprinkle with edible glitter,
Sixlets, sprinkles, and a few
nonpareils to resemble
pearls.

Seahorse

1 batch Sugar Cookie Dough (page 16)

Seahorse-shaped cookie cutter

3 pastry bags

1 Wilton #4 decorating tip

1 Wilton #104 decorating tip

1 Wilton #2 decorating tip

1 batch Buttercream Icing (page 26), divided and dyed as follows:

½ cup (120 ml) black

1 cup (240 ml) turquoise

remainder undyed (white)

White sanding sugar

❶ Follow baking instructions on page 16.

❷ Fit one pastry bag with the #4 decorating tip and fill with white icing. Fit one pastry bag with the #104 decorating tip and fill with turquoise icing. Fit one pastry bag with the #2 decorating tip and fill with black icing.

❸ Using the white icing, pipe an outline around the outer edge of the cookie and fill with horizontal lines. Dip the iced cookie in the sanding sugar.

❹ Using the turquoise icing, pipe a small ruffle on the edge of the seahorse's back to resemble a fin.

❺ Using the black icing, pipe a closed eye with one lash.

Starfish

1 batch Sugar Cookie Dough (page 16)

Starfish-shaped cookie cutter

1 pastry bag

1 Wilton #4 decorating tip

1 batch Buttercream Icing (page 26), dyed turquoise

Clear sanding sugar

❶ Follow baking instructions on page 16.

❷ Fit the pastry bag with the #4 decorating tip and fill with turquoise icing.

❸ Pipe an outline around the outer edge of the cookie and fill with horizontal lines. Dip the iced cookie in sanding sugar.

❹ Pipe one dot of icing in the center of the cookie, and two dots on each arm of the starfish.

Bananas

1 batch Sugar Cookie Dough (page 16)

Banana-shaped cookie cutter

3 pastry bags

1 Wilton #1A decorating tip

2 Wilton #2 decorating tips

1 batch Buttercream Icing (page 26), divided and dyed as follows:

   1 cup (240 ml) brown

   remainder yellow

NOTE FROM JENNY

Package these banana cookies for someone special and attach a tag that reads "I'm bananas for you!"

❶ Follow baking instructions on page 16.

❷ Fit one pastry bag with the #1A decorating tip and fill with yellow icing. Fit two pastry bags with the #2 decorating tips. Fill one with yellow icing and one with brown icing.

❸ Using the bag with the #1A decorating tip and starting at the top of the banana, pipe icing onto the cookie in a single pass: Use a minimal amount of pressure at first, then increase the pressure to widen the stripe. Try to pipe the icing all in one pass.

❹ Using the bag with the #2 decorating tip and the yellow icing, pipe a few lines down the length of the yellow stripe.

❺ Using the brown icing, pipe a little spot on each end to resemble the stem and bottom tip.

Fourth of July Marbled Stars

1 batch Sugar Cookie Dough
(page 16)

2 drops of red food coloring gel

2 drops of blue food coloring gel

Disposable gloves

Star-shaped cookie cutters
in various sizes

NOTES FROM JENNY

- *Before rolling your dough, add a couple of drops of red and blue food coloring gel to your cookie dough and knead it in for a pretty marbled effect.*
- *On a hot summer day, use these cookie stars to make delicious ice cream sandwiches with your favorite ice cream.*
- *These cookie stars make any occasion and holiday festive—just use the food coloring that feels right for the party! For example, green marbled stars complement sparkly snowflakes in a holiday display on pages 212–213.*

❶ Make four wells in the dough and place one drop of food coloring in each well. While wearing disposable gloves to protect your hands from the dye, carefully knead the food coloring gel throughout the dough, creating a marbled effect (do not knead too much or you'll just get purple dough!).

❷ Cut the dough using the cookie cutters and bake according to the directions on page 16. Let the cookies cool completely.

Pool Party

Flamingo Float

YOU WILL NEED

1 batch Sugar Cookie Dough (page 16)

Flamingo float– or swan float–shaped cookie cutter

3 pastry bags

1 Wilton #1A decorating tip

2 Wilton #3 decorating tips

1 batch Buttercream Icing (page 26), divided and dyed as follows:

½ cup (120 ml) black

½ cup (120 ml) undyed (white)

remainder pink

❶ Follow baking instructions on page 16.

❷ Fit one pastry bag with the #1A decorating tip and fill with pink icing. Fit two pastry bags with the #3 decorating tips. Fill one with black icing and the other with white icing.

❸ Using the pink icing, starting at the bottom of the neck, and using medium pressure, pipe around the underside of the flamingo and up the neck and to the head, ending just before the beak. Try to pipe in one fluid motion. Add a wing and a tail.

❹ Using the black icing, pipe an eye and a beak on the flamingo.

❺ Using the white icing, pipe a line where the beak meets the head.

Swan Float

1 batch Sugar Cookie Dough (page 16)

Swan float–shaped cookie cutter

3 pastry bags

1 Wilton #1A decorating tip

1 Wilton #3 decorating tip

1 Wilton #2 decorating tip

1 batch Buttercream Icing (page 26), divided and dyed as follows:

   ½ cup (120 ml) black

   ½ cup (120 ml) yellow

   remainder undyed (white)

NOTE FROM JENNY
Mix coconut or orange extract into your icing for a blast of summer flavor. Serve poolside with a glass of pink lemonade.

❶ Follow baking instructions on page 16.

❷ Fit one pastry bag with the #1A decorating tip and fill with white icing. Fit one pastry bag with the #3 decorating tip and fill with yellow icing. Fit one pastry bag with the #2 decorating tip and fill with black icing.

❸ Using the white icing, starting at the bottom of the neck, and using medium pressure, pipe around the underside of the swan and up the neck and to the head, ending just before the beak. Try to pipe in one fluid motion. Add a wing and a tail.

❹ Using the yellow icing, pipe a triangle for the swan's beak.

❺ Using the black icing, pipe a closed eye with one lash and a line along the top of the beak.

Unicorn Float

YOU WILL NEED

1 batch Sugar Cookie Dough (page 16)

Unicorn float–shaped cookie cutter

3 pastry bags

1 Wilton #1A decorating tip

1 Wilton #18 decorating tip

1 Wilton #2 decorating tip

1 batch Buttercream Icing (page 26), divided and dyed as follows:

   ½ cup (120 ml) black

   1 cup (240 ml) pink

   1 cup (240 ml) purple

   remainder undyed (white)

❶ Follow baking instructions on page 16.

❷ Fit one pastry bag with the #1A decorating tip and fill with white icing. Fit one pastry bag with the #18 decorating tip. Smear a line of purple icing down one side of the pastry bag and fill the rest of the bag with pink icing. This will give the icing a two-toned effect. Fit one pastry bag with the #2 decorating tip and fill with black icing.

❸ Using the white icing, starting at the bottom of the neck, and using medium pressure, pipe around the underside of the unicorn and up the neck and to the head (as on previous 2 pages). Try to pipe in one fluid motion.

❹ Using the two-toned icing and starting at the top of the head, pipe a continuous row of swirls to make a mane down onto the body. Using the same icing, pipe short curved lines to make a tail.

❺ Using the black icing, pipe a closed eye with eyelashes.

Chocolate Chip Ice Cream Sandwiches

1 batch Sugar Cookie Dough
(page 16)

1 cup (198 g) mini chocolate chips

2-inch (5-cm) round cookie cutter

Chocolate chip–vanilla ice cream

NOTE FROM JENNY

*Fill these chocolate chip mix-in
cookies with your favorite ice cream
flavor or add a pop of color by
incorporating a little food coloring gel
into the cookie dough before baking.*

❶ Mix the mini chocolate chips
into the cookie dough until
fully incorporated.

❷ Cut the dough using the
cookie cutter and bake
according to the directions
on page 16. Let the cookies
cool completely.

❸ Spread a generous amount
of ice cream on the back side
of one cookie, then top with
another cookie. Repeat for
the remaining cookies. Store
in the freezer.

Tropical Luau

Palm Tree

YOU WILL NEED

1 batch Sugar Cookie Dough
(page 16)

Palm tree–shaped cookie cutter

2 pastry bags

1 Wilton #4 decorating tip

1 Wilton #352 decorating tip

1 batch Buttercream Icing (page
26), divided and dyed into equal
amounts of the following colors:

   green

   brown

❶ Follow baking instructions on
page 16.

❷ Fit one pastry bag with the
#4 decorating tip and fill with
brown icing. Fit one pastry
bag with the #352 decorating
tip and fill with green icing.

❸ Using the brown icing, pipe
an outline around the outer
edge of the trunk and fill with
horizontal lines.

❹ Using the green icing and
starting in the center of
the palm fronds area of the
cookie, pipe fronds by making
long leaves that extend to
the end of the branches. To
do this, with the two points
of the tip held vertically, like
a bird's open beak, squeeze
and form the base of each
leaf, pull toward the end of
the branches, and gently
release the pressure to form
each point. Add a few small
fronds on top of the previous
branches.

❺ Using the brown icing, pipe
three dots of icing at the base
of the fronds to resemble
coconuts.

Hibiscus Flower

1 batch Sugar Cookie Dough (page 16)

2½-inch (6.35-cm) round cookie cutter

2 pastry bags

1 Wilton #104 decorating tip

1 Wilton #4 decorating tip

1 batch Buttercream Icing (page 26), divided and dyed as follows:

   ½ cup (120 ml) orange

   remainder pink

❶ Follow baking instructions on page 16.

❷ Fit one pastry bag with the #104 decorating tip and fill with pink icing. Fit one pastry bag with the #4 decorating tip and fill with orange icing.

❸ Using the pink icing and starting at the center of the cookie, pipe radiating lines of petals by holding the bag at an angle and exerting gentle pressure as you "ruffle" the icing, moving from the center to the outer edge.

❹ Using the orange icing, pipe radiating lines along the petals plus one curved line ending in a dot.

Pineapple

YOU WILL NEED

1 batch Sugar Cookie Dough (page 16)

Pineapple-shaped cookie cutter

2 pastry bags

1 Wilton #18 decorating tip

1 Wilton #104 decorating tip

1 batch Buttercream Icing (page 26), divided and dyed as follows:

    one-third green

    two-thirds yellow

❶ Follow baking instructions on page 16.

❷ Fit one pastry bag with the #18 decorating tip and fill with green icing. Fit one pastry bag with the #104 decorating tip and fill with yellow icing.

❸ Using the yellow icing and starting at the top of the oval area, pipe short petals to resemble the texture of a pineapple, squeezing while dragging the tip downward then releasing. Work in overlapping rows until you reach the base of the cookie.

❹ Using the green icing, pipe short lengths to resemble leaves at the top of the pineapple.

Hula Skirt

1 batch Sugar Cookie Dough
(page 16)

Grass skirt–shaped cookie cutter

3 pastry bags

1 Wilton #233 decorating tip

2 Wilton #18 decorating tips

1 batch Buttercream Icing (page 26),
divided and dyed as follows:

   ½ cup (120 ml) pink

   ½ cup (120 ml) orange

   remainder green

NOTES FROM JENNY

▸ *These tropical cookies taste great
with coconut-flavored icing.*

▸ *They are perfect for summer luaus,
end-of-the-year classroom parties,
or Hawaiian-themed parties.*

❶ Follow baking instructions on
page 16.

❷ Fit one pastry bag with
the #233 decorating tip
and fill with green icing. Fit
two pastry bags with #18
decorating tips. Fill one with
orange icing and the other
with pink icing.

❸ Using the green icing and
starting ½ inch (12 mm) from
the top edge of the cookie,
pipe gently curved vertical
lines to mimic a skirt; repeat
until the surface is covered
and the skirt has depth.

❹ Using the pink icing, pipe small
swirls to look like flowers.

❺ Using the orange icing, pipe
small stars to look like flowers.

Farmers Market Bouquet

Sunflower

YOU WILL NEED

1 batch Sugar Cookie Dough
(page 16)

2½-inch (6.35-cm) round cookie
cutter

2 pastry bags

1 Wilton #18 decorating tip

1 Wilton #1A decorating tip

1 batch Buttercream Icing
(page 26), divided and dyed
into equal amounts of the
following colors:

golden yellow

brown

NOTE FROM JENNY
*Replicate in a color palette of your
choice to coordinate with any party or
event theme.*

❶ Follow baking instructions on
page 16.

❷ Fit one pastry bag with the
#18 decorating tip and fill
with golden-yellow icing. Fit
one pastry bag with the #1A
decorating tip and fill with
brown icing.

❸ Using the golden-yellow icing
and starting ½ inch (12 mm)
from the outer edge of the
cookie, pipe individual petals
around the entire edge by
holding the bag vertically
and pulling the icing toward
the outer edge of the cookie
with even pressure.

❹ Using the brown icing,
squeeze a dollop in the
center of the cookie,
overlapping the petals.

Chrysanthemum

YOU WILL NEED

1 batch Sugar Cookie Dough (page 16)

2½-inch (6.35-cm) round cookie cutter

1 pastry bag

1 Wilton #81 decorating tip

1 batch Buttercream Icing (page 26), dyed orange

❶ Follow baking instructions on page 16.

❷ Fit the pastry bag with the #81 decorating tip and fill with orange icing.

❸ Starting ½ inch (12 mm) from the outer edge of the cookie, pipe small individual petals around the entire edge by holding the bag vertically and pulling the icing toward the outer edge of the cookie with even pressure.

❹ Move toward the center of the cookie and pipe another layer of petals over the first layer.

❺ Finish with a few petals in the center.

Carnation

1 batch Sugar Cookie Dough
(page 16)

2½-inch (6.35-cm) round cookie
cutter

1 pastry bag

1 Wilton #401 decorating tip

1 batch Buttercream Icing
(page 26), dyed dark purple

❶ Follow baking instructions on
page 16.

❷ Fit the pastry bag with the
#401 decorating tip and fill
with dark-purple icing.

❸ Starting ½ inch (12 mm) from
the outer edge of the cookie,
pipe small individual petals
around the entire edge,
pulling the icing toward the
outer edge of the cookie.

❹ Move toward the center of
the cookie and pipe another
layer of petals over the first
layer.

❺ Finish with a few petals in the
center.

Dahlia

YOU WILL NEED

1 batch Sugar Cookie Dough
(page 16)

2½-inch (6.35-cm) round cookie
cutter

1 pastry bag

1 Wilton #104 decorating tip

1 batch Buttercream Icing (page 26),
dyed purple

❶ Follow baking instructions on page 16.

❷ Fit the pastry bag with the #104 decorating tip and fill with purple icing.

❸ Starting ¼ inch (6 mm) from the outer edge of the cookie, and with the larger end of the decorating tip up, pipe individual petals by holding the bag vertically and pulling the icing straight into the center with even pressure.

❹ Move toward the center of the cookie and pipe another layer of petals over the first layer.

❺ Finish with a few petals in the center.

The Great Outdoors

Fir Tree

1 batch Sugar Cookie Dough
(page 16)

Tree-shaped cookie cutter

2 pastry bags

2 Wilton #4 decorating tips

1 batch Buttercream Icing (page 26),
divided and dyed as follows:

  2 cups brown

  remainder forest green

NOTE FROM JENNY
*This collection of cookies works
for a glamping celebration by just
swapping the icing colors—from bold
and natural hues to magical pastels.*

❶ Follow baking instructions on
page 16.

❷ Fit the pastry bags with #4
decorating tips and fill one
with brown icing and one with
forest-green icing.

❸ Using the brown icing, pipe a
tree trunk down the middle of
the tree and fill with vertical
lines.

❹ Using the forest-green icing,
pipe four rows of branches
across the tree in a wide
vertical zigzag.

Snowcapped Mountain

YOU WILL NEED

1 batch Sugar Cookie Dough
(page 16)

Small mountain-shaped cookie
cutter, or a triangle cookie cutter

1 pastry bag

1 Wilton #4 decorating tip

1 batch Buttercream Icing (page 26),
undyed (white)

① Follow baking instructions on
page 16.

② Fit the pastry bag with the
#4 decorating tip and fill with
white icing.

③ Pipe an outline around the
point of the cookie, extending
about two-thirds of the way
down, and fill with horizontal
lines.

④ "Mess" the icing up a bit to
resemble snow using an
offset spatula.

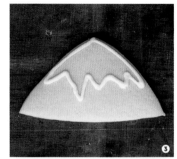

Big Foot

YOU WILL NEED

1 batch Sugar Cookie Dough (page 16)

Big Foot-shaped cookie cutter

2 pastry bags

2 Wilton #4 decorating tips

1 batch Buttercream Icing (page 26), divided and dyed as follows:

    ½ cup (120 ml) black

    remainder brown

Brown sprinkles

❶ Follow baking instructions on page 16.

❷ Fit the pastry bags with #4 decorating tips and fill one with brown icing and one with black icing.

❸ Using the brown icing, pipe an outline around the outer edge of the cookie, sparing the face, feet, and hands, and fill with horizontal lines.

❹ Dip the iced cookie in brown sprinkles.

❺ Using the brown icing, outline the face, feet, and hands and fill with lines.

❻ Using the black icing, pipe an eye onto Big Foot.

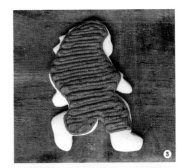

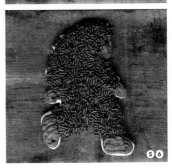

Campfire

YOU WILL NEED

1 batch Sugar Cookie Dough (page 16)

Campfire-shaped cookie cutter

2 pastry bags

1 Wilton #10 decorating tip

1 Wilton #199 decorating tip

1 batch Buttercream Icing (page 26), divided and dyed into equal amounts of the following colors:

  brown

  dark orange

❶ Follow baking instructions on page 16.

❷ Fit one pastry bag with the #10 decorating tip and fill with brown icing. Fit one pastry bag with the #199 decorating tip and fill with dark-orange icing.

❸ Using the brown icing, pipe four logs at the bottom of the cookie.

❹ Using the orange icing and starting at the top center of the logs, use medium pressure to pipe the icing upward to a point to resemble a flame. Repeat two more times.

❺ Starting in the same spot as the first layer, pipe four shorter flames on top of the previous flames.

Compass

1 batch Sugar Cookie Dough (page 16)

1½-inch (3.81-cm) round cookie cutter

3 pastry bags

1 Wilton #4 decorating tip

2 Wilton #2 decorating tips

1 batch Buttercream Icing (page 26), divided and dyed as follows:

    ½ cup (120 ml) red

    1 cup (240 ml) black

    remainder undyed (white)

❶ Follow baking instructions on page 16.

❷ Fit one pastry bag with the #4 decorating tip and fill with white icing. Fit two pastry bags with #2 decorating tips and fill one with black icing and one with red icing.

❸ Using the white icing, pipe an outline around the outer edge of the cookie and fill with horizontal lines.

❹ Using the black icing, pipe a circle around the outside edge of the cookie. Pipe directional markers and a pointer on the face of the compass.

❺ Using the red icing, pipe the tip of the pointer.

Tent

1 batch Sugar Cookie Dough
(page 16)

Tent-shaped cookie cutter

4 pastry bags

3 Wilton #4 decorating tips

1 Wilton #2 decorating tip

1 batch Buttercream Icing (page 26),
divided and dyed as follows:

  ½ cup (120 ml) gray

  1 cup (240 ml) brown

  half remaining light blue

  half remaining undyed (white)

❶ Follow baking instructions on
page 16.

❷ Fit three pastry bags with #4
decorating tips and fill one
with gray icing, one with light-
blue icing, and one with white
icing. Fit one pastry bag with

the #2 decorating tip and fill
with brown icing.

❸ Using the blue icing, follow
the shape of the cookie to
pipe an outline about ½ inch
(12 mm) from the outer edge
of the cookie. Pipe a tent
window near the center and
two lines across the middle
to create three rows on the
tent (see top photo). Fill in the
top and bottom areas with
vertical lines.

❹ Using the white icing, fill the
middle section of the tent
with vertical lines.

❺ Using the gray icing, fill in the
tent window with horizontal
lines.

❻ Using the brown icing, pipe
tent poles and supports
around the outer edge of
the cookie.

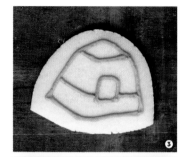

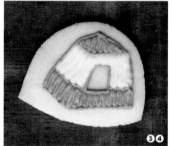

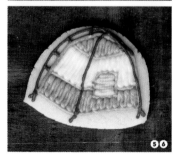

S'mores

YOU WILL NEED

1 batch Sugar Cookie Dough (page 16)

X-shaped cookie cutter

2 pastry bags

2 Wilton #4 decorating tips

1 batch Buttercream Icing (page 26), divided and dyed into equal amounts of the following colors:

   brown

   undyed (white)

❶ Follow baking instructions on page 16.

❷ Fit the pastry bags with the #4 decorating tips and fill one with brown icing and one with white icing.

❸ Using the brown icing, pipe two sticks onto the cookie in an X. To make their rough texture, slightly raise and lower your arm as you pull.

❹ Using the white icing, pipe a "marshmallow" at the end of each stick.

❺ Using the brown icing, add accents to the marshmallows to give them a "toasted" look.

Farm-Fresh Cookies

Cherries

YOU WILL NEED

1 batch Sugar Cookie Dough (page 16)

Cherry-shaped cookie cutter

2 pastry bags

1 Wilton #1A decorating tip

1 Wilton #4 decorating tip

1 batch Buttercream Icing (page 26), divided and dyed as follows:

    1 cup (120 ml) light green

    remainder red

❶ Follow baking instructions on page 16.

❷ Fit one pastry bag with the #1A decorating tip and fill with red icing. Fit one pastry bag with the #4 decorating tip and fill with light-green icing.

❸ Using the red icing, pipe two large mounds at the bottom to resemble cherries.

❹ Using the green icing, pipe stems on the top of the cherries, piping a small leaf where the two stems meet, as shown in the photo.

Corn

YOU WILL NEED

1 batch Sugar Cookie Dough (page 16)

Corn-shaped cookie cutter

2 pastry bags

1 Wilton #1A decorating tip

1 Wilton #352 decorating tip

1 batch Buttercream Icing (page 26), divided and dyed as follows:

    two-thirds golden yellow

    one-third leaf green

❶ Follow baking instructions on page 16.

❷ Fit one pastry bag with the #1A decorating tip and fill with golden-yellow icing. Fit one pastry bag with the #352 decorating tip and fill with leaf-green icing.

❸ Using the golden-yellow icing and starting at the top of the ear of corn, pipe to resemble corn kernels by pulling the tip down slightly and releasing. Continue to make slightly overlapping rows of kernels until you reach ½ inch (12 mm) from the bottom of the ear of corn.

❹ Using the leaf-green icing, pipe long leaves over the bottom row of corn to resemble the corn's husk.

Strawberry

1 batch Sugar Cookie Dough (page 16)

Strawberry-shaped cookie cutter

3 pastry bags

1 Wilton #4 decorating tip

1 Wilton #352 decorating tip

1 Wilton #2 decorating tip

1 batch Buttercream Icing (page 26), divided and dyed as follows:

    ½ cup (120 ml) undyed (white)

    half remaining red

    half remaining green

❶ Follow baking instructions on page 16.

❷ Fit one pastry bag with the #4 decorating tip and fill with red icing. Fit one pastry bag with the #352 decorating tip and fill with green icing. Fit one pastry bag with the #2 decorating tip and fill with white icing.

❸ Using the red icing, pipe an outline around the outer edge of the cookie and fill with horizontal lines.

❹ Using the green icing, pipe a few leaves at the top of the cookie.

❺ Using the white icing, randomly pipe seeds on the strawberry.

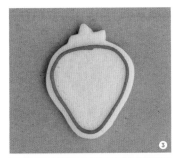

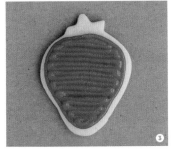

Lettuce

1 batch Sugar Cookie Dough
(page 16)

2½-inch (6.35-cm) round cookie
cutter

1 pastry bag

1 Wilton #104 decorating tip

1 batch Buttercream Icing (page 26),
dyed light green

❶ Follow baking instructions on
page 16.

❷ Fit the pastry bag with the
#104 decorating tip and fill
with light-green icing.

❸ Starting ½ inch (12 mm)
from the outer edge, hold
the decorating bag tilted at
a 45-degree angle and use
small motions to create a
ruffled, continuous spiral
around the entire edge and
overlapping as you reach the
center.

Beet

1 batch Sugar Cookie Dough (page 16)

Beet-shaped cookie cutter

2 pastry bags

1 Wilton #1A decorating tip

1 Wilton #352 decorating tip

1 batch Buttercream Icing (page 26), divided and dyed as follows:

    half dark-purple

    half green

❶ Follow baking instructions on page 16.

❷ Fit one pastry bag with the #1A decorating tip and fill with dark-purple icing. Fit one pastry bag with the #352 decorating tip and fill with green icing.

❸ Using the purple icing and starting at the base of the stems, pipe a wide zigzag tapering to the bottom of the beet, covering the cookie.

❹ Using the green icing, pipe stems, starting at the base of the beet top and working to the top of the cookie.

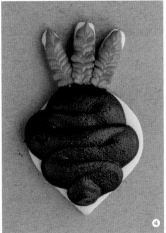

Carrot

1 batch Sugar Cookie Dough
(page 16)

Carrot-shaped cookie cutter

2 pastry bags

1 Wilton #1A decorating tip

1 Wilton #352 decorating tip

1 batch Buttercream Icing (page 26),
divided and dyed as follows:

   two-thirds orange

   one-third green

NOTES FROM JENNY

> *Fruit and veggie sugar cookies
> are a must for summer picnics or
> anytime someone asks you to bring
> a veggie tray!*

> *These cookies look great displayed
> in a wooden market crate or in a
> berry basket.*

❶ Follow baking instructions on
page 16.

❷ Fit one pastry bag with the
#1A decorating tip and fill
with orange icing. Fit one
pastry bag with the #352
decorating tip and fill with
green icing.

❸ Using the orange icing,
starting from the base of the
top, pipe a wide zigzag that
tapers to the tip of the carrot,
covering the cookie.

❹ Using the green icing, pipe
three carrot tops, starting
at the base of the carrot
top and working to the top
of the cookie. To create the
feathery look, gently raise
and lower your hand as you
pipe. Make sure the two
points of the tip look like a
bird's open vertical beak.

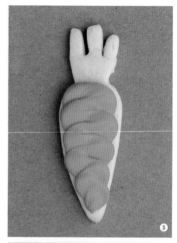

Down on the Farm

Cow

1 batch Sugar Cookie Dough
(page 16)

Cow head–shaped cookie cutter

4 pastry bags

2 Wilton #4 decorating tips

2 Wilton #1A decorating tips

1 batch Buttercream Icing
(page 26), divided and dyed
as follows:

    1½ cups (360 ml) pink

    1 cup (240 ml) black

    remainder undyed (white)

NOTE FROM JENNY

*These farm animal sugar cookies are
perfect for farm-themed birthday
parties or classroom treats. Make the
whole set or pick one of your favorite
animals.*

❶ Follow baking instructions on
page 16.

❷ Fit two pastry bags with the #4
decorating tips. Fill one with all
but about ½ cup (120 ml) of the
white icing and one with black
icing. Fit two pastry bags with the
#1A decorating tips. Fill one with
the remaining white icing and one
with pink icing.

❸ Using the bag with the #4
decorating tip and the white icing,
pipe an outline around the cow's
face, sparing the ears and nose,
and fill with horizontal lines.

❹ Using the bag with the #1A tip and
white icing, with medium pressure,
pipe two ears on the cow.

❺ Using the pink icing, pipe a big nose
at the bottom of the cow's face.

❻ Using the black icing, pipe
random spots on the cow, two
eyes, and nostrils.

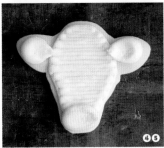

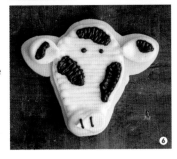

Baby Chick

1 batch Sugar Cookie Dough (page 16)

2½-inch (6.35-cm) round cookie cutter

3 pastry bags

1 coupler

3 Wilton #4 decorating tips

1 Wilton #104 decorating tip

1 batch Buttercream Icing (page 26), divided and dyed as follows:

   ½ cup (120 ml) orange

   ½ cup (120 ml) black

   remainder soft yellow

❶ Follow baking instructions on page 16.

❷ Fit one pastry bag with a coupler, the #4 decorating tip and fill with soft-yellow icing. Fit one pastry bag with the #4 decorating tip and fill with orange icing. Fit one pastry bag with the #4 decorating tip and fill with black icing.

❸ Using the bag with the #4 decorating tip and the soft-yellow icing, pipe an outline around the outer edge of the cookie and fill with horizontal lines.

❹ Using the bag with the yellow icing, replace the #4 decorating tip for the #104 decorating tip and pipe wings on both sides of the chick's body.

❺ Using the orange icing, pipe three short lines to make feet on the bottom of the chick and a small V for a beak near the center.

❻ Using the black icing, pipe two dots for eyes.

Sheep

1 batch Sugar Cookie Dough (page 16)

Sheep head–shaped cookie cutter

4 pastry bags

2 Wilton #1A decorating tips

1 Wilton #18 decorating tip

1 Wilton #4 decorating tip

1 batch Buttercream Icing (page 26), divided and dyed as follows:

    ½ cup (120 ml) pink

    ½ cup (120 ml) black

    remainder undyed (white)

❶ Follow baking instructions on page 16.

❷ Fit one pastry bag with the #1A decorating tip and fill with white icing. Fit one pastry bag with the #1A decorating tip and fill with pink icing. Fit one pastry bag with the #18 decorating tip

and fill with more of the white icing. Fit one pastry bag with the #4 decorating tip and fill with black icing.

❸ Using the white icing bag with the #1A decorating tip, starting at the center of the sheep's face, use a good amount of pressure to make a spiral, leaving about ½ inch (12 mm) around the outside clear. Pipe small petals to form the sheep's ears.

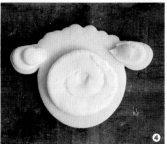

❹ Using the pink icing, pipe smaller petals atop each ear.

❺ Using the bag with the #18 decorating tip, with a swirling motion, pipe around the sheep's face and then across the top of its head.

❻ Using the black icing, pipe the sheep's eyes, nose, and mouth.

Pig

1 batch Sugar Cookie Dough (page 16)

Pig head–shaped cookie cutter

2 pastry bags

1 Wilton #1A decorating tip

1 Wilton #4 decorating tip

1 batch Buttercream Icing (page 26), divided and dyed as follows:

    ½ cup (120 ml) black

    remainder pink

❶ Follow baking instructions on page 16.

❷ Fit one pastry bag with the #1A decorating tip and fill with pink icing. Fit one pastry bag with the #4 decorating tip and fill with black icing.

❸ Using the pink icing and applying firm pressure, pipe a circle of icing on the face, sparing the ears and the very center. Carefully smooth the icing flat with an offset spatula.

❹ Pipe each ear by squeezing a dollop of icing around the top and then the bottom of each ear to resemble a teardrop shape. Pipe a wide oval snout.

❺ Using the black icing, pipe two dots for eyes and two lines for nostrils.

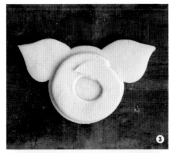

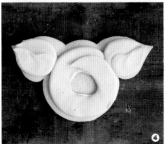

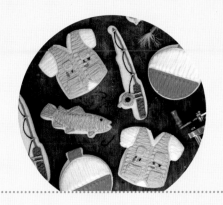

FALL

Back to School

Chalkboard

YOU WILL NEED

1 batch Sugar Cookie Dough (page 16)

4-inch (10-cm) long rectangular cookie cutter

5 pastry bags

4 Wilton #4 decorating tips

1 Wilton #3 decorating tip

1 batch Buttercream Icing (page 26), divided and dyed as follows:

    ½ cup (120 ml) green

    ½ cup (120 ml) red

    1 cup (240 ml) brown

    ½ cup (120 ml) undyed (white)

    remainder black

NOTES FROM JENNY

▶ *Personalize these chalkboard cookies with the teacher's name or class.*

▶ *Fill a vintage lunch box with cookies placed in cupcake liners or use a small chalkboard as a tray to display cookies.*

❶ Follow baking instructions on page 16.

❷ Fit four pastry bags with the #4 decorating tips. Fill one with red, one with brown, one with white, and one with black icing. Fit one pastry bag with the #3 decorating tip and fill with green icing.

❸ Using the brown icing, pipe an outline around the outer edge of the cookie.

❹ Using the black icing, fill in the outlined area with horizontal lines.

❺ Using the white icing, pipe a math equation or spelling words on the chalkboard. Pipe a small piece of chalk at the bottom.

❻ Using the red icing, pipe a small dot with a stem to resemble an apple.

❼ Using the green icing, pipe a small leaf on the apple.

Pencil

1 batch Sugar Cookie Dough (page 16)

Pencil-shaped cookie cutter

5 pastry bags

5 Wilton #4 decorating tips

1 batch Buttercream Icing (page 26), divided and dyed as follows:

  ½ cup (120 ml) gray

  ½ cup (120 ml) black

  1 cup (240 ml) pale pink

  1 cup (240 ml) light brown

  remainder golden yellow

❶ Follow baking instructions on page 16.

❷ Fit the pastry bags with the #4 decorating tips and fill them with each of the icings.

❸ Using the pink icing, pipe an outline around the edge of the eraser.

❹ Using the gray icing, pipe two horizontal lines against the pink eraser to resemble the metal ferrule on a pencil.

❺ Using the golden-yellow icing, pipe an outline around the outer edge of the middle of the pencil.

❻ Using the light-brown icing, outline the tip of the pencil. Using the black icing, pipe the pencil lead.

❼ Using the brown icing, fill in the tip of the pencil.

❽ Using the golden-yellow icing, fill in the body of the pencil using vertical lines.

❾ Using the pink icing, fill in the eraser of the pencil using vertical lines.

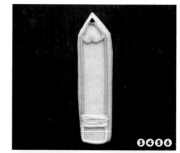

Apple

1 batch Sugar Cookie Dough (page 16)

Apple-shaped cookie cutter

3 pastry bags

3 Wilton #4 decorating tips

1 batch Buttercream Icing (page 26), divided and dyed as follows:

    1 cup (240 ml) green

    1 cup (240 ml) brown

    remainder red

❶ Follow baking instructions on page 16.

❷ Fit the pastry bags with the #4 decorating tips. Fill one with red icing, one with green icing, and one with brown icing.

❸ Using the red icing, pipe an outline around the outer edge of the apple and fill with horizontal lines.

❹ Using the brown icing, pipe an apple stem at the top of the cookie. Use more pressure at the beginning and the end to add width.

❺ Using the green icing, pipe an outline of a leaf and fill in with horizontal lines.

Notebook Paper

YOU WILL NEED

1 batch Sugar Cookie Dough (page 16)

4-inch (10-cm) long rectangular cookie cutter

3 pastry bags

1 Wilton #4 decorating tip

2 Wilton #3 decorating tips

1 batch Buttercream Icing (page 26), divided and dyed as follows:

    1 cup (240 ml) blue

    1 cup (240 ml) red

    remainder undyed (white)

❶ Follow baking instructions on page 16.

❷ Fit one pastry bag with the #4 decorating tip and fill with white icing. Fit two pastry bags with #3 decorating tips. Fill one with red icing and one with blue icing.

❸ Using the white icing, pipe an outline around the outer edge of the cookie and fill with horizontal lines.

❹ Using the blue icing, pipe lines across the cookie to resemble notebook paper lines.

❺ Using the red icing, pipe a vertical line ½ inch (12 mm) from the left edge and an "A+" in the middle of the paper.

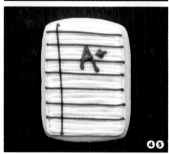

Crayons

YOU WILL NEED

1 batch Sugar Cookie Dough (page 16)

Crayon-shaped cookie cutter

4 pastry bags

4 Wilton #4 decorating tips

1 batch Buttercream Icing (page 26), divided and dyed into equal amounts of the following colors:

   red

   blue

   green

   black

❶ Follow baking instructions on page 16.

❷ Fit the pastry bags with the #4 decorating tips. Fill each one with one color of the icing.

❸ Using the blue icing, pipe an outline around the outer edge of the cookie and fill with horizontal lines. Repeat on one-third of the cookies

❹ Repeat with the red icing and the green icing on the rest of the cookies, icing one third with red icing and one third with green icing.

❺ Using the black icing, pipe two zigzag lines toward the top and bottom of the cookies. Pipe an oval in the middle.

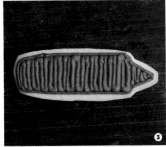

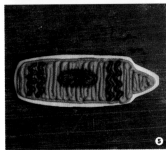

Touchdown Treats

End Zone

YOU WILL NEED

1 batch Sugar Cookie Dough
(page 16)

3-inch (7.5-cm) round cookie cutter

2 pastry bags

2 Wilton #4 decorating tips

1 batch Buttercream Icing (page 26),
divided and dyed as follows:

    1 cup (240 ml) undyed (white)

    remainder green

Rainbow nonpareils

❶ Follow baking instructions on page 16.

❷ Fit the pastry bags with the #4 decorating tips. Fill one with green icing and one with white icing.

❸ Using the white icing, pipe an outline around the top half of the cookie and fill with horizontal lines. Dip it in rainbow nonpareils to cover.

❹ Using the green icing, pipe an outline around the bottom half of the cookie and fill with horizontal lines.

❺ Using the white icing, pipe a goal post on the field in front of the crowd.

Football

YOU WILL NEED

1 batch Sugar Cookie Dough
(page 16)

Football-shaped cookie cutter

2 pastry bags

2 Wilton #4 decorating tips

1 batch Buttercream Icing (page 26),
divided and dyed as follows:

    ½ cup (120 ml) undyed (white)

    remainder brown

❶ Follow baking instructions on
page 16.

❷ Fit the pastry bags with #4
decorating tips. Fill one with
brown icing and the other
with white icing.

❸ Using the brown icing, pipe
an outline around the outer
edge of the cookie and fill
with vertical lines.

❹ Using the white icing, pipe
lines on the cookie to
resemble stitching. Pipe two
curved lines on the ends.

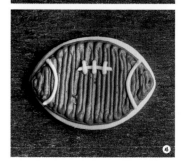

Team Spirit

Basketball

1 batch Sugar Cookie Dough (page 16)

2½-inch (6.35-cm) round cookie cutter

2 pastry bags

2 Wilton #4 decorating tips

1 batch Buttercream Icing (page 26), divided and dyed as follows:

  1 cup (240 ml) brown

  remainder orange

NOTES FROM JENNY

- *Bake these sports-themed cookies for team parties or playoffs.*
- *Decorate these treats in your favorite team's colors or pipe your favorite player's number or team's name on the balls.*
- *For directions for football cookies, see page 146.*

❶ Follow baking instructions on page 16.

❷ Fit two pastry bags with the #4 decorating tips. Fill one with brown icing and one with orange icing.

❸ Using the orange icing, pipe an outline around the outer edge of the cookie.

❹ Using the brown icing, pipe curved lines to divide the sections of the basketball.

❺ Using the orange icing, fill in each section separately using a back-and-forth motion.

Tennis Ball

YOU WILL NEED

1 batch Sugar Cookie Dough (page 16)

2½-inch (6.35-cm) round cookie cutter

2 pastry bags

2 Wilton #4 decorating tips

1 batch Buttercream Icing (page 26), divided and dyed as follows:

   1 cup (240 ml) undyed (white)

   remainder yellow

Clear sanding sugar

❶ Follow baking instructions on page 16.

❷ Fit the pastry bags with the #4 decorating tips. Fill one with white icing and one with yellow icing.

❸ Using the yellow icing, pipe an outline around the outer edge of the cookie and fill with vertical lines.

❹ Dip the iced cookie in the sanding sugar.

❺ Using the white icing, pipe a curved line on the tennis ball to resemble the seams.

Soccer Ball

1 batch Sugar Cookie Dough (page 16)

2½-inch (6.35-cm) round cookie cutter

2 pastry bags

2 Wilton #4 decorating tips

1 batch Buttercream Icing (page 26), divided and dyed into equal amounts of the following colors:

  black

  undyed (white)

❶ Follow baking instructions on page 16.

❷ Fit the pastry bags with the #4 decorating tips. Fill one with black icing and the other with white icing.

❸ Using the black icing, pipe lines to divide the soccer ball into pentagonal and hexagonal shapes, using the photo as a guide. Fill in the pentagons with horizontal lines.

❹ Using the white icing, fill the hexagons with horizontal lines.

Volleyball

YOU WILL NEED

1 batch Sugar Cookie Dough
(page 16)

2½-inch (6.35-cm) round cookie
cutter

1 pastry bag

1 Wilton #4 decorating tip

1 batch Buttercream Icing (page
26), undyed (white)

❶ Follow baking instructions on
page 16.

❷ Fit the pastry bag with the
#4 decorating tip and fill with
white icing.

❸ Pipe an outline around the
outer edge of the cookie and
fill with vertical lines.

❹ Pipe lines on the volleyball to
resemble the seams, using the
photo as a guide.

Edible Flower Cookies

YOU WILL NEED

1 batch Sugar Cookie Dough
(page 16)

1 cup (40 g) chopped dried edible
flowers (nasturtiums, pansies, rose
petals, lavender)

2-inch (5-cm) round cookie cutter

Buttercream Icing Glaze (page 27)

NOTES FROM JENNY

- *Try melting lemon-flavored buttercream and glaze the tops of these flower cookies for extra flavor.*
- *Create cookie tags for gifts! Use a tag-shaped cookie cutter; to make the small hole in the tag for a ribbon, use the back end of a decorating tip.*

❶ Set one quarter cup of the chopped flowers aside. Mix the remaining flowers into the cookie dough until fully incorporated.

❷ Cut the sugar cookie dough using the cookie cutter, then press some of the reserved flowers into the tops. Bake according to the directions on page 16.

❸ Brush on the Buttercream Icing Glaze while the cookies are still warm.

A Cookie Cake for Any Occasion

1 batch Sugar Cookie Dough
(page 16)

Pie slice–shaped cookie cutter

2 pastry bags

1 Wilton #1A decorating tip

1 Wilton #18 decorating tip

1 batch Buttercream Icing (page 26),
dyed light pink

Confetti quinns

Confetti sprinkles

❶ Follow baking instructions on
page 16.

❷ Fit one pastry bag with the
#1A decorating tip and fill
with two-thirds of the icing.
Fit one pastry bag with the
#18 decorating tip and fill
with the remaining icing.

❸ Using the bag with the #1A
decorating tip and starting at
the wide end of the cookie,
pipe a zigzag to fully cover the
cookie, being careful not to
go over the edge. Repeat with
twenty-seven more cookies.

❹ Using an angled spatula,
smooth the icing on seven of
the cookies. Sprinkle some
confetti and sprinkles along
the wide edge of the cookies.
Using the bag with the #18 tip,
pipe a border using a swirling
motion along the wide end
of the cookies, overlapping
the confetti.

❺ Assemble the "cake" as
follows: stack three cookies
atop each other, then top
with the confetti-decorated
cookie. Arrange the seven
stacks on a cake stand to
resemble a cake.

Join the Circus

Cotton Candy

YOU WILL NEED

1 batch Sugar Cookie Dough (page 16)

Ice-cream-cone–shaped cookie cutter

2 pastry bags

1 Wilton #4 decorating tip

1 Wilton #18 decorating tip

1 batch Buttercream Icing (page 26), divided and dyed as follows:

    one-third undyed (white)

    two-thirds blue

NOTES FROM JENNY

- *Display circus cookies on a tray of shelled peanuts or popcorn! Stack ticket rolls to create height on a dessert table and top with cookies.*
- *Mix and match these cookies for a variety of celebrations. I like popcorn and ticket cookies for movie night, or the cotton candy cookie in a sweet shop theme.*
- *Substitute pink icing to make classic pink cotton candy!*

❶ Follow baking instructions on page 16.

❷ Fit one pastry bag with the #4 decorating tip and fill with white icing. Fit one pastry bag with the #18 decorating tip and fill with blue icing.

❸ Using the white icing, pipe a narrow V shape on the bottom half of the cookie to resemble the cotton candy holder. Fill with horizontal lines.

❹ Using the blue icing, pipe a cloud-shaped outline on the top half of the cookie and fill using a squiggly motion to resemble cotton candy.

Ticket

1 batch Sugar Cookie Dough
(page 16)

4-inch (10-cm) long rectangular
cookie cutter

2 pastry bags

2 Wilton #4 decorating tips

1 batch Buttercream Icing (page 26),
divided and dyed as follows:

　1 cup (240 ml) black

　remainder red

❶ Follow baking instructions on page 16.

❷ Fit the pastry bags with #4 decorating tips. Fill one with red icing
and one with black icing.

❸ Using the red icing, pipe an outline around the outer edge of the
cookie and fill with vertical lines. Pipe a rectangle in the center of
the cookie.

❹ Using the black icing, write the word "ticket" in the center of the
rectangle. Pipe dashed lines on the short edges of the cookies.

Ring of Fire

1 batch Sugar Cookie Dough
(page 16)

Donut-shaped cookie cutter

3 pastry bags

1 Wilton #4 decorating tip

2 Wilton #352 decorating tips

1 batch Buttercream Icing (page 26),
divided and dyed into equal amounts
of the following colors: red, orange,
golden yellow

❶ Follow baking instructions on page 16.

❷ Fit one pastry bag with the #4 decorating tip and fill with red
icing. Fit two pastry bags with the #352 decorating tips and fill
one with orange icing and one with golden-yellow icing.

❸ Using the red icing, pipe a circle ¼ inch (6 mm) from the outside
edge of the cookie.

❹ Using the orange icing, create flames along the red circle, leaving
some spaces. To do this, squeeze to form the base of each
flame and then gently release pressure to form each point. Using
the golden-yellow icing, fill in the gaps with more flames.

Popcorn

1 batch Sugar Cookie Dough (page 16)

Popcorn-shaped cookie cutter

3 pastry bags

1 coupler

3 Wilton #10 decorating tips

1 Wilton #4 decorating tip

1 batch Buttercream Icing (page 26), divided and dyed as follows:

    one-quarter golden yellow

    one-quarter remaining red

    remaining undyed (white)

❶ Follow baking instructions on page 16.

❷ Fit two pastry bags with the #10 decorating tips. Fill one bag with white icing and one with golden-yellow icing. Fit one pastry bag with a coupler and the #4 decorating tip and also fill with red icing.

❸ Using the bag with the #4 decorating tip, pipe an outline around the outer edge of the bottom two-thirds of the cookie.

❹ Using the white icing, pipe four vertical lines equally spaced within the outlined area.

❺ Switch the decorating tip on the red icing to the #10 decorating tip. Pipe three vertical lines between the white icing lines so that the area is completely filled.

❻ Using the golden-yellow icing, dot dollops to cover the top of the cookie to resemble popcorn.

Circus Tent

1 batch Sugar Cookie Dough (page 16)

Circus tent–shaped cookie cutter

4 pastry bags

3 Wilton #4 decorating tips

1 Wilton #2 decorating tip

1 batch Buttercream Icing (page 26), divided and dyed as follows:

  ½ cup (120 ml) golden yellow

  remainder divided equally: red, blue, and undyed (white)

1. Follow baking instructions on page 16.

2. Fit three pastry bags with the #4 decorating tips. Fill one with red icing, one with white icing, and one with blue icing. Fit one pastry bag with the #2 decorating tip and fill with golden-yellow icing.

3. Using the red icing, pipe an outline around the outer edge of the top of the cookie and across the middle. Pipe 4 lines radiating out from the top point to the middle line to create five spaces on the awning. Pipe the bottom half of the tent as shown in the photo.

4. Fill the middle and outer wedges of the top and the middle vertical spaces on the bottom with horizontal lines.

5. Using the white icing, fill in the blank spaces of the awning and tent bottom with horizontal lines. Leave the entrance to the tent blank.

6. Using the blue icing, pipe two curtains and fill with horizontal lines. Pipe a scalloped bunting along the top of the tent's awning. Pipe a dot at the very top of the tent.

7. Using the golden-yellow icing, pipe little lights along the edge of the tent awning and at the points of the curtains.

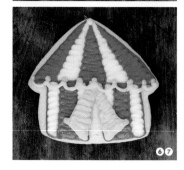

Elephant

1 batch Sugar Cookie Dough (page 16)

Elephant-shaped cookie cutter

4 pastry bags

1 Wilton #4 decorating tip

3 Wilton #2 decorating tips

1 batch Buttercream Icing (page 26), divided and dyed as follows:

    ½ cup (120 ml) black

    1 cup (240 ml) golden yellow

    1 cup (240 ml) blue

    remainder gray

❶ Follow baking instructions on page 16.

❷ Fit one pastry bag with the #4 decorating tip and fill with gray icing. Fit three pastry bags with the #2 decorating tips and fill one with blue icing, one with golden-yellow icing, and one with black icing.

❸ Using the gray icing, pipe an outline around the outer edge of the cookie and fill with vertical lines. Pipe an ear on the cookie and fill with horizontal lines.

❹ Using the blue icing, pipe a square on the elephant's back and fill with horizontal lines to resemble a blanket.

❺ Using the golden-yellow icing, pipe a band along and just within the outer edge of the blanket and add a few dots along the bottom.

❻ Using the black icing, pipe an eye on the elephant.

Woodland

....

Deer

....

YOU WILL NEED

1 batch Sugar Cookie Dough
(page 16)

Deer-shaped cookie cutter

5 pastry bags

4 Wilton #4 decorating tips

1 Wilton #18 decorating tip

1 batch Buttercream Icing (page 26),
divided and dyed as follows:

    ½ cup (120 ml) undyed (white)

    ½ cup (120 ml) black

    ½ cup (120 ml) dark brown

    remainder light brown

NOTE FROM JENNY

*These cookies are perfect for your
next woodland-themed party or an
adorable addition to a baby shower.*

FIR TREE

*See directions in The Great Outdoors
section on page 117.*

....

❶ Follow baking instructions on
page 16.

❷ Fit four pastry bags with the #4
decorating tips. Fill one with
light-brown icing, one with black
icing, one with dark-brown icing,
and one with half of the white
icing. Fit one pastry bag with the
#18 decorating tip and fill with
the remaining white icing.

❸ Using the light-brown icing, pipe
an outline around the outer edge
of the cookie, sparing the tail
area, and fill with horizontal lines.

❹ Using the white icing with the #4
decorating tip, add a few spots
on the deer's rump.

❺ Using the black icing, pipe a
closed eye.

❻ Using the dark-brown icing, dot
a small nose onto the deer.

❼ Using the bag with the #18 tip,
pipe a fluffy white tail on the deer.

Mushroom

1 batch Sugar Cookie Dough
(page 16)

Mushroom-shaped cookie cutters
in various sizes

3 pastry bags

3 Wilton #4 decorating tips

1 batch Buttercream Icing (page 26),
divided and dyed as follows:

  1 cup (240 ml) undyed (white)

  half remaining brown

  half remaining red

❶ Follow baking instructions on
page 16.

❷ Fit each pastry bag with the
#4 decorating tips. Fill one
with white icing, one with
brown icing, and one with red
icing.

❸ Using the brown icing, pipe
an outline of the stem of
the mushroom and fill with
horizontal lines.

❹ Using the red icing, pipe an
outline around the outer
edge of the top of the cookie
and fill with horizontal lines.

❺ Using the white icing, pipe
various size dots on the tops
of the mushrooms.

Hedgehog

1 batch Sugar Cookie Dough
(page 16)

Hedgehog-shaped cookie cutter

3 pastry bags

2 Wilton #4 decorating tips

1 Wilton #2 decorating tip

1 batch Buttercream Icing (page 26),
divided and dyed as follows:

   ½ cup (120 ml) black

   1 cup (240 ml) light brown

   remainder dark brown

Chocolate sprinkles

❶ Follow baking instructions on
page 16.

❷ Fit two pastry bags with the
#4 decorating tips. Fill one
with dark-brown icing and the
other with light-brown icing.
Fit one pastry bag with the
#2 decorating tip and fill with
black icing.

❸ Using the dark-brown icing,
pipe an outline around the
edges of the cookie, sparing
the head and legs, and fill with
vertical lines. Dip the iced
cookie in chocolate sprinkles.

❹ Using the light-brown icing,
pipe an outline around the
edge of the head and legs and
fill with horizontal lines.

❺ Using the black icing, pipe
an eye and nose on the
hedgehog.

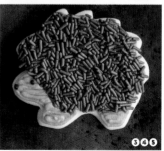

Pumpkin Patch

1 batch Sugar Cookie Dough
(page 16)

Pumpkin-shaped cookie cutters in
various sizes

3 pastry bags

1 Wilton #4 decorating tip

2 Wilton #1A decorating tips

1 batch Buttercream Icing (page 26),
divided and dyed as follows:

   1 cup (240 ml) brown

   half remaining orange

   half remaining undyed (white)

NOTE FROM JENNY

*Pumpkin-shaped sugar cookies will
always be my favorite since they were
the shape that started it all. From the
original cookie recipe to a pumpkin
spice–flavored cookie, these seasonal
treats are still a fan favorite.*

❶ Follow baking instructions on
page 16.

❷ Fit one pastry bag with the
#4 decorating tip and fill with
brown icing. Fit two pastry bags
with #1A decorating tips and fill
one with orange icing and one
with white icing.

❸ Using the orange icing, pipe
an outline around the outer
edge of half of the cookies,
sparing the stem, and fill with
wide, curved vertical lines.

❹ Using the white icing, pipe
an outline around the outer
edge of the remaining cookies,
sparing the stem, and fill with
wide, curved vertical lines.

❺ Using the brown icing, pipe an
outline of a small stem on the
top of each pumpkin and fill in.

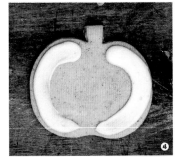

Salty-Sweet Cookies

1 batch Sugar Cookie Dough
(page 16)

1½ cups (165 g) chopped
chocolate-covered pretzels

1½-inch (3.81-cm) square cookie
cutter

Milk chocolate candy melts

NOTES FROM JENNY

▶ *These salty-sweet cookies have
just the right amount of crunch and
are delicious drizzled in chocolate.*

▶ *Mix it up by swapping white
chocolate for milk chocolate or
colored candy melts to add a pop
of color.*

❶ Reserve ¼ cup (30 g) of the
chocolate-covered pretzels.
Mix the remaining pretzels
into the cookie dough until
fully incorporated.

❷ Follow baking instructions on
page 16.

❸ Melt the candy melts in a
microwave-safe bowl on 30
percent power for 30-second
increments until melted.

❹ Using a honey dipper, drizzle
the chocolate over the
cookies and sprinkle with the
reserved chocolate-covered
pretzels.

Happy Halloween

Ghost

YOU WILL NEED

1 batch Sugar Cookie Dough
(page 16)

2 pastry bags

1 Wilton #4 decorating tip

1 Wilton #18 decorating tip

1 batch Buttercream Icing (page 26),
divided and dyed as follows:

   ½ cup (120 ml) black

   remaining undyed (white)

NOTES FROM JENNY

▶ *Try decorating cookie treat bags
with themed sprinkles or use classic
confetti quinns.*

▶ *Serve at costume parties or at
school Halloween-themed events.*

❶ Follow baking instructions on
page 16.

❷ Fit one pastry bag with the
#18 decorating tip and fill with
white icing. Fit one pastry bag
with the #4 decorating tip
and fill with black icing.

❸ Using the white icing, pipe
an outline around the outer
edge of the cookie and fill
with swirls.

❹ Using the black icing, pipe
eyes and a mouth on the
ghost.

Black Cat

YOU WILL NEED

1 batch Sugar Cookie Dough
(page 16)

Halloween cat–shaped cookie
cutter

1 Wilton #4 decorating tip

1 batch Buttercream Icing (page 26),
dyed black

Black sanding sugar

❶ Follow baking instructions on
page 16.

❷ Fit one pastry bag with the
#4 decorating tip and fill with
black icing.

❸ Pipe an outline around the
outer edge of the cookie and
fill with horizontal lines.

❹ Dip the iced cookie in the
sanding sugar.

Trick-or-Treat Bucket

YOU WILL NEED

1 batch Sugar Cookie Dough
(page 16)

Candy corn–shaped cookie cutter

3 pastry bags

3 Wilton #4 decorating tips

1 batch Buttercream Icing (page 26),
divided and dyed as follows:

    ½ cup (120 ml) undyed (white)

    1 cup (240 ml) black

    remaining orange

Halloween-themed sprinkles

❶ Follow baking instructions on page 16.

❷ Fit the pastry bags with the #4 decorating tips. Fill one with white icing, one with black icing, and one with orange icing.

❸ Using the orange icing, pipe an outline around the bottom two-thirds of the cookie and fill with horizontal lines.

❹ Using the white icing, pipe a small line across the top of the orange bucket.

❺ Using the black icing, pipe an outline around the top third of the cookie to resemble a trick-or-treat bucket handle. Pipe eyes, nose, and a mouth on the orange section.

❻ Carefully place a line of sprinkles along the white line on top of the trick-or-treat bucket.

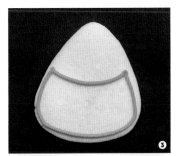

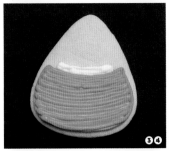

Pumpkin Cookie Pie

YOU WILL NEED

1 batch Sugar Cookie Dough
(page 16)

Pie slice–shaped cookie cutter

3 pastry bags

1 Wilton #4 decorating tip

1 Wilton #104 decorating tip

1 Wilton #18 decorating tip

1 batch Buttercream Icing (page 26),
divided and dyed as follows:

   ½ cup (120 ml) undyed (white)

   half remaining ivory

   half remaining orange

Cinnamon

NOTE FROM JENNY
*These cookies taste great with
pumpkin-pie spice mixed into the
dough and pumpkin extract mixed
into the icing for a realistic fall taste!*

❶ Follow baking instructions on
page 16.

❷ Fit one pastry bag with the
#4 decorating tip and fill

with orange icing. Fit one
pastry bag with the #104 tip
and fill with ivory icing. Fit
one pastry bag with the #18
decorating tip and fill with
white icing.

❸ Using the orange icing, pipe
an outline around the outer
edge of the cookie, sparing a
½-inch (12-mm) band at the
wide end. Fill with horizontal
lines.

❹ Using the ivory icing and
holding the bag vertically
with the larger side of the tip
closest to the cookie, pipe a
ruffle to resemble a piecrust
at the wide end of the cookie.

❺ Sprinkle a small amount of
cinnamon onto the cookie.

❻ Using the white icing and
holding the bag vertically,
use a circular motion to
place a dollop in the center
to resemble whipped cream.

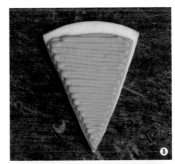

Gone Fishin'

Bobber

YOU WILL NEED

1 batch Sugar Cookie Dough
(page 16)

Ornament-shaped cookie cutter

2 pastry bags

2 Wilton #4 decorating tips

1 batch Buttercream Icing (page
26), divided and dyed into equal
amounts of the following colors:

undyed (white)

red

NOTE FROM JENNY

*Display these cookies on a dessert
table or package for gifting in a
vintage tackle box.*

❶ Follow baking instructions on
page 16.

❷ Fit the pastry bags with the
#4 decorating tips. Fill one
with white icing and one with
red icing.

❸ Using the white icing, pipe
an outline around the outer
edge of the top half of the
cookie, sparing the top notch,
and fill with vertical lines.

❹ Using the red icing, pipe an
outline around the outer
edge of the bottom half
of the cookie and fill with
vertical lines. Outline the very
tip of the bobber and fill with
vertical lines.

Fishing Vest

1 batch Sugar Cookie Dough (page 16)

Vest-shaped cookie cutter

7 pastry bags

2 Wilton #4 decorating tips

5 Wilton #2 decorating tips

1 batch Buttercream Icing (page 26), divided and dyed as follows:

½ cup (120 ml) red

½ cup (120 ml) blue

½ cup (120 ml) yellow

½ cup (120 ml) orange

½ cup (120 ml) black

1 cup (240 ml) undyed (white)

remainder light green

❶ Follow baking instructions on page 16.

❷ Fit two bags with the #4 decorating tips. Fill one with white icing and one with green

icing. Fit five pastry bags with the #2 decorating tips and fill each with one of the remaining colors of the icing.

❸ Using the white icing, pipe an outline around the sleeves and fill with horizontal lines.

❹ Using the green icing, pipe a vest outline on the remainder of the cookie. To create the appearance of a zippered vest, pipe two lines down the center. Fill in the two sides with horizontal lines. Outline and fill four pockets atop the vest.

❺ Using the additional colors of icing, "hang" (pipe) a little bobber and lures from the bottom of the top two pockets using the photos at right and on page 176 as a guide.

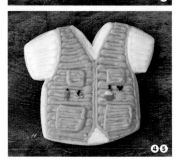

Fishing Pole

1 batch Sugar Cookie Dough (page 16)

Fishing pole–shaped cookie cutter

4 pastry bags

2 Wilton #4 decorating tips

2 Wilton #3 decorating tips

1 batch Buttercream Icing (page 26), divided and dyed into equal amounts of the following colors:

brown

red

gray

black

❶ Follow baking instructions on page 16.

❷ Fit two pastry bags with the #4 decorating tips and fill one with brown icing and one with red icing. Fit two pastry bags with the #3 decorating tips and fill one with gray icing and one with black icing.

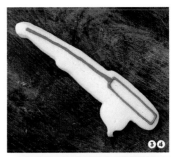

❸ Using the brown icing, pipe an outline of the rod handle and fill it with horizontal lines.

❹ Using the red icing, pipe a gently curved line for the pole.

❺ Using the gray icing, pipe a round reel and attach it to the rod handle with two lines.

❻ Using the black icing, make a large dot in the center of the reel, and pipe arcs that meet the pole to resemble the line.

❼ Using the gray icing, pipe short lines across the pole where the arcs meet the pole.

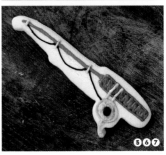

Fish

1 batch Sugar Cookie Dough (page 16)

Fish-shaped cookie cutter

3 pastry bags

1 Wilton #4 decorating tip

1 Wilton #3 decorating tip

1 Wilton #2 decorating tip

1 batch Buttercream Icing (page 26), divided and dyed as follows:

    ½ cup (120 ml) black

    one-third remaining light blue

    two-thirds remaining gray

❶ Follow baking instructions on page 16.

❷ Fit one pastry bag with the #4 decorating tip and fill with gray icing. Fit one pastry bag with the #3 decorating tip and fill with light-blue icing. Fit one pastry bag with the #2 decorating tip and fill with black icing.

❸ Using the gray icing, pipe an outline around the outer edge of the body of the fish and fill with vertical lines.

❹ Using the light-blue icing, pipe an outline around the fins and fill them in with diagonal or horizontal lines.

❺ Using the black icing, pipe an eye on the fish.

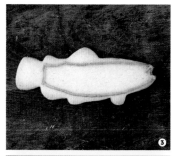

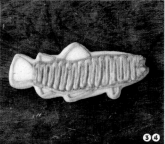

WINTER

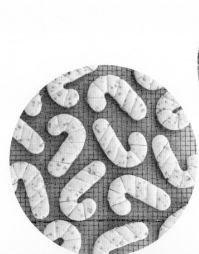

Sweet Jam Cookies

1 batch Sugar Cookie Dough (page 16)

2-inch (5-cm) scalloped round cookie cutter

Mini alphabet-shaped cookie cutters or shapes

Confectioners' sugar, for dusting

1 cup jam

NOTES FROM JENNY

- *This is a twist on the traditional Linzer cookie using my classic dough recipe.*
- *These sweet jam-filled cookies can be personalized with initials, dates, or words of endearment.*
- *Fill these cookies with a seasonal jam to complement an upcoming holiday or time of year.*
- *For a cute baby shower treat, set cookies on a tray, spelling out "Welcome, Baby" and place in a basket!*

❶ Cut the sugar cookie dough using the scalloped cookie cutter. On half of the cookies, cut out letters or shapes in their centers. Bake according to the directions on page 16. Let the cookies cool completely.

❷ Place the cookies with the cut-out motifs on a cookie sheet and sift confectioners' sugar over them. Turn the remaining cookies flat side up and spoon ½ teaspoon of jam into the center, spreading it slightly. Top with the sugar-dusted cookies.

Layered Berry Cakes

1 batch Sugar Cookie Dough
(page 16)

2-inch (5-cm) round cookie cutter

1 pastry bag

1 Wilton #1A decorating tip

¼ cup (60 ml) raspberry jam

1 batch Buttercream Icing (page 26),
undyed (white)

Mixed fresh berries, rinsed and
dried, or frozen berries

NOTE FROM JENNY
*For a hint of lemon, add lemon extract
to the cookie dough before baking for
enhanced flavor.*

❶ Follow baking instructions on
page 16.

❷ Thoroughly mix the raspberry
jam into the icing. Fit the
pastry bag with the #1A
decorating tip and fill.

❸ Pipe a swirl of icing onto one
cookie, top with another
cookie, and repeat until you
have three cookies stacked
with raspberry icing.

❹ Decorate with fresh or frozen
berries.

Outer Space

Astronaut

YOU WILL NEED

1 batch Sugar Cookie Dough
(page 16)

Gingerbread man–shaped cookie
cutter

2 pastry bags

2 Wilton #4 decorating tips

1 batch Buttercream Icing (page 26),
divided and dyed as follows:

  one-third gray

  two-thirds undyed (white)

NOTES FROM JENNY

▶ *Use a gingerbread man cookie
cutter for an astronaut and keep
stars simple by just dipping in gold
sugar.*

▶ *Planets are quick to make by
smoothing the icing with an offset
spatula.*

❶ Follow baking instructions on
page 16.

❷ Fit the pastry bags with the
#4 decorating tips. Fill one
with white icing and one with
gray icing.

❸ Using the white icing, pipe
an outline around the outer
edge of the cookie and fill
with horizontal lines. Pipe
the seams of the coat and
pants using the white icing,
following the examples in the
photos at right and opposite.

❹ Using the gray icing, pipe an
outline for the helmet window
and fill with horizontal lines.
Pipe buttons and lines across
the chest.

Planets

1 batch Sugar Cookie Dough (page 16)

1- and 2-inch (2.5- and 5-cm) round cookie cutters

4 pastry bags

4 Wilton #4 decorating tips

1 batch Buttercream Icing (page 26), divided and dyed into equal amounts of the following colors:

 blue

 undyed (white)

 orange

 gray

❶ Follow baking instructions on page 16.

❷ Fit each pastry bag with a #4 decorating tip and fill with each of the icings.

❸ On one-third of the cookies, using the blue icing, pipe an outline around the outer edge of the cookies and fill with lines.

❹ Using the gray icing, pipe three small dots onto the cookies. Using an offset spatula, blend the two icings together.

❺ Using the gray icing, pipe two horizontal lines across the planets to resemble rings.

❻ On one-third of the cookies, using the gray icing, pipe an outline around the outer edge of the cookies and fill with lines.

❼ Using the orange, white, and blue icings, pipe horizontal lines across the cookies. Using an offset spatula, blend the icings together.

❽ On one-third of the cookies, using the gray icing, pipe an outline around the outer edge of the cookies and fill with lines. Using an offset spatula, gently smooth the icing.

❾ Using the blue icing, pipe three spots on the planet to resemble land.

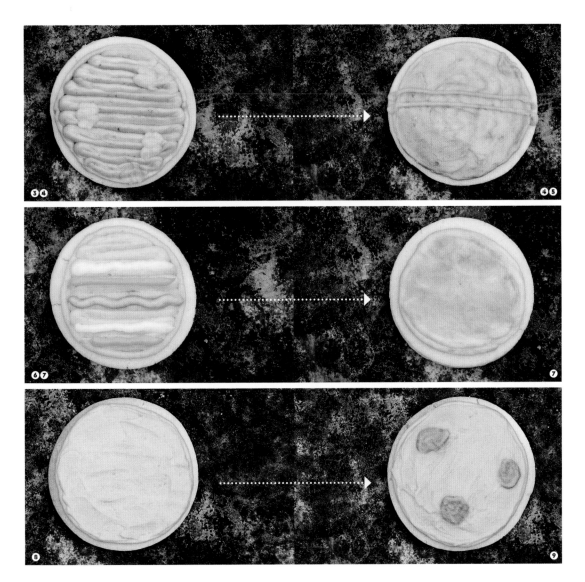

Star

YOU WILL NEED

1 batch Sugar Cookie Dough
(page 16)

Star-shaped cookie cutters in
various sizes

1 pastry bag

1 Wilton #4 decorating tip

1 batch Buttercream Icing (page 26),
dyed golden yellow

Clear sanding sugar

❶ Follow baking instructions on
page 16.

❷ Fit the pastry bag with the
#4 decorating tip and fill with
golden-yellow icing.

❸ Pipe an outline around the
outer edge of the cookie and
fill with diagonal lines. Dip the
iced cookie in sanding sugar.

Home Sweet Home

Front Door

YOU WILL NEED

1 batch Sugar Cookie Dough
(page 16)

4-inch (10-cm) long rectangular
cookie cutter

3 pastry bags

2 Wilton #4 decorating tips

1 Wilton #352 decorating tip

1 batch Buttercream Icing (page 26),
divided and dyed as follows:

    ½ cup (120 ml) black

    1 cup (240 ml) green

    remainder undyed (white)

NOTES FROM JENNY

- ➤ *Personalize these doormat cookies with the family's last name.*
- ➤ *Deliver in a vintage bread pan lined with a new kitchen towel.*

❶ Follow baking instructions on page 16.

❷ Fit two pastry bags with the #4 decorating tips. Fill one with white icing and one with black icing. Fit one pastry bag with the #352 decorating tip and fill with green icing.

❸ Using the white icing, pipe an outline around the outer edge of the cookie and fill with horizontal lines. Pipe four rectangles on the door to resemble panels.

❹ Using the black icing, pipe a door handle.

❺ Using the green icing, pipe a small ring of leaves on the top half of the door to create a wreath. Add another row of leaves inside the previous ring, overlapping slightly.

Doormat

1 batch Sugar Cookie Dough (page 16)

2½-inch (6.35-cm) long rectangular cookie cutter

2 pastry bags

1 Wilton #4 decorating tip

1 Wilton #3 decorating tip

1 batch Buttercream Icing (page 26), divided and dyed as follows:

   one-third black

   two-thirds brown

❶ Follow baking instructions on page 16.

❷ Fit one pastry bag with the #4 decorating tip and fill with brown icing. Fit one pastry bag with the #3 decorating tip and fill with black icing.

❸ Using the brown icing, pipe an outline around the outer edge of the cookie and fill with vertical lines.

❹ Using the black icing, pipe the word "Welcome" or the homeowner's name on the cookie. Pipe an outline around the edge of the cookie, leaving a space near the words as shown in the photo.

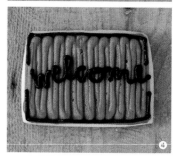

Cranberry Pistachio Cookies

YOU WILL NEED

½ cup (70 g) chopped dried cranberries

½ cup (62 g) chopped pistachios

1 batch Sugar Cookie Dough (page 16)

2-inch (5-cm) oval-shaped cookie cutter

❶ Mix the cranberries and pistachios into the cookie dough until fully incorporated.

❷ Follow baking instructions on page 16.

❸ Stack and tie with a ribbon for gift-giving.

NOTE FROM JENNY
Tie these cranberry pistachio cookies with twine or ribbon for pretty gifting or add to a holiday cookie gift box.

Winter Wonderland

YOU WILL NEED

1 batch Sugar Cookie Dough
(page 16)

Snowflake-shaped cookie cutters
in various sizes and shapes

3 pastry bags

2 Wilton #3 decorating tips

1 Wilton #18 decorating tip

1 batch Buttercream Icing (page 26),
divided and dyed as follows:

   one-third red

   two-thirds undyed (white)

White sanding sugar

NOTES FROM JENNY
- *Try adding peppermint extract to the buttercream icing for extra wintery flavor.*
- *Arrange these cookies on a round platter to form an edible wreath or package individually and attach to holiday gifts.*
- *Dust the finished cookies with powdered sugar!*

❶ Follow baking instructions on page 16.

❷ Fit two pastry bags with the #3 decorating tips. Fill one with red icing and one with a portion of the white icing. Fit one pastry bag with the #18 decorating tip and fill with the remaining white icing.

❸ Using the red icing, pipe lines to resemble snowflakes on some of the cookies.

❹ Using the bag with the #3 decorating tip and the white icing, pipe lines to resemble snowflakes on some of the cookies as shown in the photos opposite and on the next pages.

❺ Using the bag with the #3 decorating tip and the white icing, pipe an outline on some of the cookies and fill with lines. Pipe lines atop the icing in either red or white icing using either the #3 or #18 decorating tips. (For various decorating ideas, see pages 198–199.) Dip some of the iced cookies in white sanding sugar.

Cookies 'n' Cream Sandwich Cookies

1 batch Sugar Cookie Dough
(page 16)

3 cups (330 g) crushed chocolate
sandwich cookies

2-inch (5-cm) round cookie cutter

1 batch Buttercream Icing (page 26),
undyed (white)

NOTES FROM JENNY

▶ *Crush chocolate sandwich cookies
and mix into my classic Sugar
Cookie Dough, then up the ante
by sandwiching the cookies with
cookies 'n' cream icing and roll in
crushed cookies.*

▶ *Give the cookies a festive flavor by
adding peppermint extract to the
icing.*

❶ Mix 1 cup (110 g) of the crushed chocolate cookies into the
cookie dough until fully incorporated. Cut the dough using the
cookie cutter and bake according to the directions on page
16. Let the cookies cool completely.

❷ Mix 1½ cups (165 g) of the crushed chocolate cookies into the
icing.

❸ Dollop a generous amount of icing onto the back of one
cookie, then make a cookie sandwich by placing another
cookie, face up, atop the icing.

❹ Place the remaining ½ cup (55 g) of the crushed chocolate
cookies in a shallow bowl. Roll the edges of the sandwich in
the crushed chocolate cookies.

O Christmas Tree

1 batch Sugar Cookie Dough (page 16)

2 drops forest green food coloring gel

Star-shaped cookie cutters in various sizes

Disposable gloves

Small amount of Buttercream Icing (page 26), undyed (white)

Confectioners' sugar, for dusting

NOTES FROM JENNY

- *Add a little green food coloring gel to the dough before baking to give the tree a realistic look or leave as is for a traditional-cookie look.*
- *The number and sizes of stars will depend on the shape of the tree you want. Start by cutting 8–12 stars in diminishing sizes and experiment!*

❶ Make two wells in the dough and place one drop of food coloring gel in each well. While wearing disposable gloves to protect your hands from the dye, carefully knead the food coloring gel throughout the dough, creating a marbled effect (do not knead too much or the cookies will be solid green!).

❷ Cut the dough using the cookie cutters and bake according to the directions on page 16. Let the cookies cool completely.

❸ Stack the cookies on top of one another, beginning with the largest cookies on the bottom. Alternate the rotation of each of the cookies and adhere them with a small dab of icing in the center of each one.

❹ Stand the smallest star upright at the top, holding it in place with a dab of icing.

❺ Sprinkle the entire cookie tree with a generous dusting of confectioners' sugar.

Holiday Lights

YOU WILL NEED

1 batch Sugar Cookie Dough
(page 16)

3¼-inch (8.25-cm) lightbulb-
shaped cookie cutter

6 pastry bags

1 Wilton #4 decorating tip

5 Wilton #12 decorating tips

1 batch Buttercream Icing (page
26), divided and dyed as follows:

   1 cup (240 ml) gray

   1 cup (240 ml) red

   1 cup (240 ml) orange

   1 cup (240 ml) blue

   1 cup (240 ml) green

   1 cup (240 ml) yellow

Small angled spatula

NOTE FROM JENNY
*Coordinate the colors of these cookies
to match any holiday or occasion for a
truly festive treat!*

❶ Follow baking instructions on page 16.

❷ Fit one pastry bag with the #4 decorating tip and fill with gray icing. Fit the remaining five pastry bags with the #12 decorating tips. Fill one with red icing, one with orange icing, one with blue icing, one with green icing, and one with yellow icing.

❸ Using the gray icing, fill in the "base" of the cookie with back-and-forth horizontal lines to create the ridges of a lightbulb base.

❹ Using the red icing, cover the "lightbulb" area of the cookie. With the small angled spatula, carefully brush the bulb icing on the cookie to give it a little bit of dimension.

❺ Repeat steps 3 and 4 with the rest of colors, until you have created an array of colorful lightbulbs.

Santa's Treat

1 batch Sugar Cookie Dough (page 16)

2½-inch (6.35-cm) square cookie cutter

4 pastry bags

1 Wilton #47 decorating tip

3 Wilton #4 decorating tips

1 batch Buttercream Icing (page 26), divided and dyed as follows:

   ½ cup (120 ml) black

   ¼ cup (60 ml) white

   ¼ cup (60 ml) yellow

   Remainder red

NOTE FROM JENNY

On Christmas Eve, make a treat for Santa by setting out these cookies on a holiday-themed plate with a cup of milk.

❶ Follow baking instructions on page 16.

❷ Fit one pastry bag with the #47 decorating tip and fill with black icing. Fit the remaining pastry bags with the #4 decorating tips. Fill one with white icing, one with yellow icing, and one with red icing.

❸ Using the red icing, pipe an outline around the outer edge of the cookie and fill with horizontal lines.

❹ Using the black icing, pipe Santa's black belt across the center of the cookie.

❺ Using the yellow icing, pipe a square on the middle of the belt to create a belt buckle.

❻ Using the white icing, make two dots above the belt and two dots below the belt to resemble buttons.

Jolly Snowmen

1 batch Sugar Cookie Dough
(page 16)

2½-inch (6.35-cm) round cookie
cutter

3 pastry bags

1 Wilton #1A decorating tip

1 Wilton #2 decorating tip

1 Wilton #3 decorating tip

1 batch Buttercream Icing (page 26),
divided and dyed as follows:

   ½ cup (120 ml) black

   ½ cup (120 ml) orange

   remainder undyed (white)

NOTE FROM JENNY
*Give these snowmen cookies a holiday
flavor by adding peppermint extract
to the icing before decorating.*

❶ Follow baking instructions on
page 16.

❷ Fit one pastry bag with the
#1A decorating tip and fill
with white icing. Fit one
pastry bag with #2 decorating
tip and fill with the black icing.
Fit one pastry bag with the
#3 decorating tip and fill with
orange icing.

❸ Using the white icing, pipe a
large dollop onto the cookie
to cover the entire surface. If
your icing ends up shaped like
a chocolate kiss, gently tap
the cookie on the counter to
encourage the icing to settle.

❹ Using the black icing, pipe the
snowman's eyes and mouth.

❺ Using the orange icing, pipe a
nose to resemble a carrot.

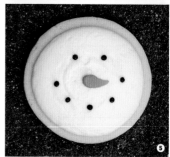

Peppermint Candy Canes

YOU WILL NEED

½ cup (115 g) crushed candy canes

1 batch Sugar Cookie Dough
(page 16)

Candy cane–shaped cookie cutter

Twine

NOTES FROM JENNY

- *The variations of these cookies are endless, from spreading peppermint-flavored icing between two cookies for a cookie sandwich treat to piping stripes of my basic Buttercream Icing on top.*

- *Tie a pretty bow of green-and-white twine around the cookies. Present on a tray sprinkled with peppermint candies.*

❶ Mix the crushed candy canes into the cookie dough until fully incorporated. Cut the sugar cookie dough using the cookie cutter and bake according to the directions on page 16. Let the cookies cool completely.

❷ Stack and tie with twine for simple gifting.

Party Animals

1 batch Sugar Cookie Dough
(page 16)

Camel-, giraffe-, and bear-shaped
cookie cutters

2 pastry bags

2 Wilton #4 decorating tips

1 batch Buttercream Icing (page 26),
divided and dyed into equal
amounts of the following colors:

   pink

   undyed (white)

Rainbow nonpareils

NOTES FROM JENNY

- *Inspired by nostalgic circus-animal cookies, these buttercream animals can be quickly decorated by sprinkling them with rainbow nonpareils.*
- *Change it up for New Year's Eve! Cut a triangle out of fondant to make a fun party hat. Premade fondant can be purchased at many craft stores!*

❶ Follow baking instructions on page 16.

❷ Fit two pastry bags with the #4 decorating tips. Fill one with pink icing and one with white icing.

❸ On half of the cookies, use the white icing to pipe an outline around the edge of each cookie and fill with horizontal or vertical lines. On the other half of the cookies, use the pink icing to pipe an outline and fill.

❹ Sprinkle the iced cookies with rainbow nonpareils.

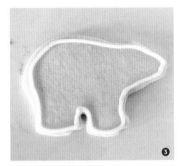

Happy New Year!

Clock

1 batch Sugar Cookie Dough (page 16)

2½-inch (6.35-cm) round cookie cutter

2 pastry bags

1 Wilton #4 decorating tip

1 Wilton #2 decorating tip

1 batch Buttercream Icing (page 26), divided and dyed as follows:

    one-third black

    two-thirds undyed (white)

❶ Follow baking instructions on page 16.

❷ Fit one pastry bag with the #4 decorating tip and fill with white icing. Fit one pastry bag with the #2 decorating tip and fill with black icing.

❸ Using the white icing, pipe an outline around the outer edge of the cookie and fill with horizontal lines.

❹ Using the black icing, pipe a circle around the outside. Pipe numbers or Roman numerals along the circle and in the center pipe an hour and minute hand.

Party Hat

YOU WILL NEED

1 batch Sugar Cookie Dough (page 16)

Party hat-shaped cookie cutter

3 pastry bags

2 Wilton #4 decorating tips

1 Wilton #18 decorating tip

1 batch Buttercream Icing (page 26), divided and dyed as follows:

   ½ cup (120 ml) undyed (white)

   remainder black

Gold sanding sugar

Gold confetti quinns

Clear, white, and gold sprinkles

NOTE FROM JENNY

- Gold or silver? Blue or purple? Create your own custom sprinkle mix to coordinate with the occasion—from holidays to birthdays!

- Mix cocoa powder into the buttercream for a natural nearly black color, or swap the black icing on the hats for a different color to coordinate with your party.

❶ Follow baking instructions on page 16.

❷ Fit two pastry bags with the #4 decorating tips. Fill one with white icing, and one with a portion of the black icing. Fit another pastry bag with the #18 decorating tip and fill with the remainder of the black icing.

❸ Using the white icing, pipe a small circle for the top of the hat and fill in. Dip in sanding sugar.

❹ Using the black icing, pipe an outline around the outer edge of the cookie and fill with horizontal lines. Sprinkle the bottom third of the hat with confetti quinns and sprinkles.

❺ Using the bag with the #18 decorating tip, pipe a ruffled line of icing along the bottom edge to resemble the cuff of the hat.

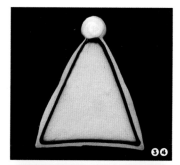

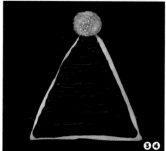

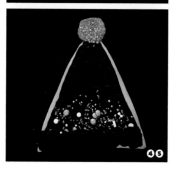

Acknowledgments

To everyone at Harper Design: Thank you for the opportunity to bring this book to life! A special thanks to Dani Segelbaum, who shared my vision and believed in the potential of this amazing project, and Elizabeth Smith, who helped complete an incredible book with confidence and cheerful energy.

To my agent, Coleen O'Shea, who saw a promising future in Jenny Cookies several years ago: Thank you for your continued guidance and wisdom.

To Donna Diegel, who saw me through this process once again, this time from across the globe: It was so enjoyable to work with you.

To my cookie squad at Jenny Cookies Bake Shop: You've come along with me and grown a party of one into an unstoppable team. Rachel Miller, you have been instrumental in the growth of Jenny Cookies Bake Shop and a valuable resource when it comes to building and expanding our brand. We complement each other's talents so well; I can't wait to see where it takes us! Jeannie Sahatdijan— not only one of the hardest working women I've ever known, but one of the most talented. Thank you for your consistent willingness to jump in and do what needs to be done while offering endless amounts of encouraging support.

To Kelly Bowie: It's not often that you have a friend who wholeheartedly supports, encourages, and celebrates life alongside of you. You are a rare gem, my friend. You bring so much more than pretty pictures. Thank you for always capturing the magic.

To Ally and Hudson: You two are the loves of my life. You continue to make me proud every day. I love you more than words can say.

To Dan Keller, my biggest fan and my toughest critic: Thank you for always encouraging me to be better than I was yesterday.

And to my family, friends, and the amazing cookie community across social media: a heartfelt thank-you. I'm so grateful for your continued support and encouragement. Never forget— always save room for cookies!

Index

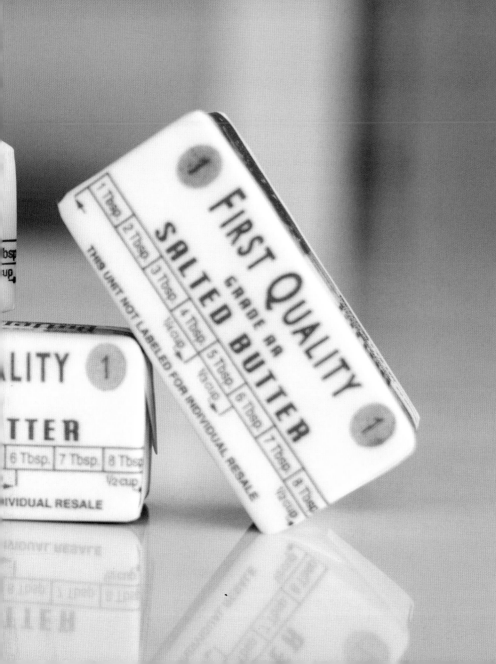

About the Author

JENNY KELLER is the creator of JennyCookies.com, the author of the cookbook *Eat More Dessert*, and the owner of the destination bakery Jenny Cookies Bake Shop in Lake Stevens, Washington.

Jenny's ideas are simple, timeless, and creative. From desserts to everyday entertaining, Jenny lends inspiration and encouragement to others for their own events and everyday celebrations. Her style, designs, and expertise have been seen in *Country Living, Better Homes & Gardens, People, US Weekly, Brides, Flea Market Style*, and more. When she's not creating for JennyCookies.com, Jenny styles and creates content for brands such as Wilton, Pottery Barn Kids, Warner Bros., Fresh, Bath & Body Works, McCormick, JOANN, and more to connect consumers with their products. She is also well known for her work with numerous celebrities such as Tori Spelling, Tiffani Thiessen, Sarah Michelle Gellar, and many of ABC's *The Bachelor* and *The Bachelorette* contestants.

Jenny lives in Seattle with her husband, Dan, and their two children, Ally and Hudson.